Pause for Thought

Pause for Thought

Twenty-five Stories for Assembly
with Follow-up Work

Molly Cheston

Blackie

Blackie & Son Ltd.,
Bishopbriggs, Glasgow G64 2NZ
450 Edgware Road, London W2 1EG

© Molly Cheston 1976
First Published 1976
ISBN 0 216 90262 2

Printed in Great Britain by Robert MacLehose & Co. Ltd
Printers to the University of Glasgow

Preface

There are two main areas in which I hope teachers will find this collection useful: first as stories to tell in assembly, and second as a basis for discussion, improvisation and creative writing in the classroom.

Assembly The school population today includes representatives of many different faiths as well as most branches of the Christian church. So when I found that, as Pastoral Tutor, I had to take morning assembly, I decided the wisest course was to leave the teaching of religion to the experts and concentrate on finding the basic standards of behaviour common to all men of goodwill no matter what, if any, church or temple they attend.

There is no denying that a strong story catches and holds the attention of boys and girls of all ages better than most things, but everyone dislikes a story with a moral! In this collection I have tried to walk the tight-rope between being too obviously "moral" and merely being an entertainer. In the contents list, I have tried to give an indication of the theme of each story. Though originally written for pupils in a Secondary School, the stories can also be used for Middle and Upper Primary Schools. It all depends on the manner of the "telling".

For the most part the stories are based on true incidents. (Obvious exceptions are the legends.) This, I find, gives them an impact quite lacking in a fictional account. They are written colloquially to be read, or preferably told, in an easy, informal way. A sense of timing will help enormously, but, as every good story teller knows, to be over-dramatic invites mockery.

The order in which the stories are printed is a reference only to the length of time each takes to read aloud. This naturally varies with the reader and the audience, but is usually between five and ten minutes. The shorter stories form roughly the first two thirds of the book, and the longer ones are at the end.

If used in a traditional assembly, the period for quiet thought could be prefaced with the suggestion: "Let us close our eyes and think." The "thoughts" can then slip naturally into prayer. Alternatively, the "close our eyes" suggestion can be omitted.

Classwork Each story is followed by suggested ways in which it might be used as a basis for discussion and creative work. Of course, all teachers will have their own ideas and may use all, part or none of the suggestions. I find it is best to be flexible, so that different classes can follow whatever line they find most interesting and rewarding.

The method in which work is tackled often varies but the order usually followed is:

1. The story, possibly followed by a period of quiet thought, probably without any prompting by the teacher.
2. Class comment and talk to draw out the theme or themes of the story. Sometimes comments come bubbling out immediately the story is over so that one can plunge straight into discussion and cut the reflection time.
3. "Tell us about"—any facts or relevant experiences members of the class can share.
4. Discussion on broader issues suggested by the story.
5. "Find out"—this section can be used either for research as a class or as a task for homework.
6. Creative work—either individual work, such as creative writing or drawing, or group work, such as dramatic improvisation or the preparation of a tape or pamphlet.

Situations suitable for improvised drama often arise from the personal experience of the pupils, but, if it doesn't, valuable experience can be gained by creating their own situations and working these out in dramatic form. One of the great obstacles to creative writing is the limited experience of the pupils which results in a lack of any basis on which to found their writing. The experience of "living" a situation through in improvised drama and seeing the effect of their words and actions on other people can sometimes prove unexpectedly fruitful.

However teachers use this book, I hope they will find that it saves them some of that precious commodity, time.

I should like to thank: the authors and publishers who have allowed me to base some of my stories on their material; The Royal National Life-boat Institution; The Chief Constable of Norfolk and his staff, especially Inspector Statham; and my colleagues, past and present, whose comments have invariably been helpful.

M.C.

Contents

Escape from the Tower

When Queen Anne died in 1714, the British parliament invited the Protestant George of Hanover to be king, and he became King George I. But there were many people who did not want George to be king; they would have preferred the Roman Catholic James, son of the exiled James I. James' supporters were called "Jacobites".

In the year 1715, the Jacobites rose in rebellion against King George, but were soon routed by his army. One of the Jacobite leaders captured was William Maxwell, Earl of Nithsdale. He was taken to London where he was tried, found guilty and sentenced to death.

The Earl of Nithsdale had a wife, Winifred, who was at home in Dumfries in Scotland when she heard of her husband's capture. At once she set out for London to beg for his life. In those days the roads were very poor. Often in winter they were quite impassable, but Winifred was determined to get to London, nearly four hundred miles away. She travelled by stagecoach, on horseback and even, sometimes, on foot, through mud, fog and some of the worst snowstorms in living memory. It took her three weeks to get to London, and almost the first news she heard when she arrived was that her husband's execution had been brought forward. He was now to be beheaded the very next day.

Undeterred she decided to go to the king himself and beg him to show mercy. It wasn't easy for a known Jacobite to get into the palace, but she managed it and threw herself on her knees before the king, begging him to show mercy to the conquered man who could no longer harm him. King George turned his back and walked away. Desperately the Countess clutched his arm; the king walked on dragging her after him on her knees until the guards forcibly removed her.

It seemed that every hope had failed, but Winifred decided that if no one else would get her husband out of prison she must do it herself. At first it seemed an impossible task; escape from the Tower of London was unheard of and the Earl was very well guarded. Besides, even if he did get out of the Tower, that was only the beginning of the Earl's difficulties. The moment the escape became known, the whole of England would be looking for him.

Winifred had heard that the Venetian ambassador was sympathetic towards the Jacobites but dared not help them openly because his government could not afford to offend the king. However, he might be persuaded to turn a blind eye if his household suddenly acquired a new footman. He might even take that footman with him when he went to France, which he planned to do very soon.

On the eve of execution, friends of the condemned man were allowed to visit him to say goodbye. Winifred had two women friends whom she persuaded to help her, although they knew they would be severely punished if they were discovered. The Earl was a short, slightly-built man. Winifred planned to disguise him as a woman and somehow trick the warders into thinking he was one of the female visitors who was so overcome by her grief that she wept, with her handkerchief to her face, all the way from the death cell to the main gate of the Tower.

The authorities would certainly suspect that the women visitors were responsible for the escape, but they could do nothing without proof. Leaving one of the women behind in the cell in the Earl's place would give them proof enough, so, although Winifred and *two* women went into the cell, Winifred and *three* women had to come out of it! Somehow the guards had to be distracted so that they did not notice either the extra woman going out or the empty cell when Winifred left.

Somehow Winifred managed it. By shuttling her friends in and out of the cell on one excuse after another, she so confused the warders that she got all three "women" out. She then carried on a conversation with herself in the cell, so that the listening warders thought she was talking to her husband, and the others had time to get safely away. At last, she herself left, telling the guards that the Earl needed a few minutes alone to recover from the emotion of parting.

It was not long before the alarm was raised, but the Earl of Nithsdale had vanished and, despite all efforts to find him, he managed to escape from the country. For nearly thirty years he lived a peaceful life in Rome with his wife and children.

Winifred Maxwell, a slight, delicate woman of thirty-four, had defeated King George, his parliament and his army because she refused to say, "It's impossible."

Assembly

Let us close our eyes and think. Let us think about ourselves. How do we tackle difficult tasks? How often do we say, "I can't do it, it's impossible"? Sometimes it is so much easier to give up than to go on trying. Winifred Maxwell was not prepared to give in. She drove her frail body through snow and storm when many strong men would have given up. She faced a seemingly impossible task and refused to say, "There is no more I can do". She went on looking for different ways and means until she finally succeeded.

Let us think of times when we have said, "I can't,"—times when perhaps we should have said, "I will try harder, again and again until I succeed."

Classwork

Tell us about: *a.* a time when you have given up trying to do something because it was too difficult or you couldn't be bothered.

b. anyone you know who is inclined to give up too easily (e.g. in gym or homework).

Discuss: At the time of the story people were executed for a number of different offences. At the present time we have abolished the death sentence for most crimes. If there were to be a referendum on the reintroduction of the death penalty for murder, how would you vote?

Find out: What happened to the other two Jacobite leaders captured with the Earl of Nithsdale (Derwentwater and Kenmure)?

Group improvisation: Divide into groups of 8–10. Appoint a leader who will direct your play but not take part himself.

After escaping from the Tower, the Earl of Nithsdale disguised himself as a footman and accompanied the Venetian ambassador on his journey to the coast and then on to a ship bound for France.

The alarm was raised long before they reached the coast, and King George's men searched everywhere for Nithsdale. Traffic to the coast was particularly suspect and the Earl must have had a number of narrow escapes.

Devise a short play (3–5 mins) about one of these adventures.

Individual work: *a.* Write an essay on "Nothing that is worth having can be had easily".

b. Write a story about an accident which happens to a couple (husband/wife; son/mother; brother/sister; etc.). One of the pair fights to save the other's life.

The Story of Gelert

This story has come down to us in various forms for many hundreds of years. The earliest version came from India, but the version I am going to tell you is about a man who lived in Britain. He was a great man and a great prince who has an important part in the history of Britain. His name was Llewellyn.

If you ever go on holiday to North Wales you may visit a place called Beddgelert. It was here, over six hundred years ago, that Llewellyn lived.

In those days, much of Britain was still covered with thick forests. Lots of animals lived in the forests—deer, wild boar and fierce wolves.

Like other noblemen of his time, Prince Llewellyn liked to go hunting and he had many dogs to help him find the wild animals he needed to feed his family and servants. These dogs were big, strong wolf-hounds, not like our pet dogs of today. There were no Pekes or poodles then, and even an Alsatian would have looked meek and mild beside a wolf-hound. The Prince's favourite hound was a dog called Gelert, who adored his master and followed him everywhere.

One day Prince Llewellyn decided to go hunting, but he knew that fierce wolves had been seen in the forest near the castle. He was anxious for the safety of his baby son, for hungry wolves had been known to find their way into houses. So he told Gelert to stay behind and guard the boy.

In those days there were no cots with high sides to keep a baby safe. Probably the tiny prince lay on a wooden bench covered with a sheepskin. The dog, Gelert, lay on the rush-strewn floor beside the bed. Prince Llewellyn went off happily, feeling sure his son would be safe with Gelert.

Several hours later the Prince returned and went into the room where he had left the baby—the child was nowhere to be seen, and there was no sign of Gelert.

Then the Prince saw that the rushes beside the bed were spattered with blood. Horrified, he thought, "Has Gelert gone wild and carried off the baby?"

Frantically he searched the room, then grasped his sword and dashed outside shouting for his servants to follow him. Bloodstains on the ground showed him the way. With fear clutching his heart Llewellyn ran, following the trail, drawn sword in his hand. Then he saw the dog.

Slowly Gelert came towards his master—and there was blood dripping from his jaws. With a cry of rage, Llewellyn sprang forward and thrust his sword deep into the hound's side, killing it instantly.

Hardly pausing for a moment the Prince pressed on, following the bloodstains, until he rounded a corner and saw, on the ground, not the torn and mangled body of his baby son, but the freshly-killed carcase of a huge wolf.

While the Prince stared in bewilderment, his servants came panting up to tell him his baby son had been found, curled up safe and unharmed in the rugs at the bottom of his bed.

Far from harming the child, Gelert had attacked a fierce wolf which had somehow found its way into the baby's room. They had fought and the noise had probably wakened the baby, who had crawled off the bed and into the pile of rugs where he had fallen fast asleep.

The wolf had escaped and Gelert had chased it, eventually catching and killing it. The dog had been coming back to the castle when Prince Llewellyn had met and killed it. It was the wolf's blood on Gelert's jaws, not the baby Prince's.

Filled with remorse, Prince Llewellyn buried his faithful hound and named the place "Beddgelert", which means "the grave of Gelert", a name it still carries, more than 600 years later.

Assembly

Let us close our eyes and think how anger destroys. We can all lose our tempers; we can all also learn to control them. When we let our tempers master us, we cannot think clearly and may say or do something we will be very sorry for afterwards. This is what happened to Llewellyn.

Even when our anger *seems* to be justified, it is wise to hold back and not say or do the cruel, unkind things which cannot be forgotten. Llewellyn had every reason to *think* his anger was justified, and he was wrong—we can be wrong too.

Classwork

Tell us about: *a.* what happens to you when you get really angry.

        b. any incident you have heard of or read about when a person's anger has destroyed something or hurt someone he or she loves.

Discuss: *a.* Which particular jobs or professions call for great self control?

        b. "It is absurd for anyone who cannot control himself to think of trying to control anyone else—therefore such a person has no right to have any children."

Find out: what is meant by "battered babies" and "battered wives".

Group improvisation: Divide into groups of about 6 people. Discuss among yourselves situations (preferably from your own experience) where someone might get very angry and do something he or she bitterly regrets. Decide which situation you will use, and act a play about it. Plan it carefully to build to the final climax. End the play with the line, "What have I done?"

Individual work: Write a story which starts, "A wave of fury swept over me as . . ."

3

Six Brave Men and a Queen

Calais is the nearest foreign port to England. When King Edward III was at war with France he decided he had to have a good port where he could land his supplies and reinforcements. Calais was the obvious choice, but Calais was very strongly fortified. Rather than throw away his men's lives by storming the city, Edward laid siege to the town in order to starve its citizens into surrender.

Both sides settled down to a long, hard winter. Inside Calais food became short, and plump burghers became thinner and thinner. Pet dogs and cats disappeared, and even rats were hunted for food.

With the arrival of spring came news that King Philip of France was coming with a huge army to save the people of Calais. There were only two routes he could take to reach the town, and Edward effectively blocked them both. After several attempts, the French king realized he could not get through, so he retreated, leaving Calais to its fate.

King Edward waited with growing impatience. He had expended a great deal of time and money, as well as English lives, on Calais. Now, without hope of French help, the city would either have to starve to death or surrender. The city Governor tried to make terms but Edward insisted on unconditional surrender. Unconditional surrender meant letting loose the most savage destruction on the town and its people. A number of the King's friends tried to persuade him to be more merciful, as he did not usually want revenge. At last Edward agreed to think again, but he still insisted that an example must be made of Calais so that no other town would resist so long.

"Tell the Governor to send me six of his most important citizens to do with as I please," he commanded. "Let them walk here to me in bare feet, with rope halters round their necks, and carrying the keys of the city and the castle in their hands."

When the Governor announced the terms to the citizens there was a moment of horrified silence—the rope halters could only mean one thing. Then Eustache de St Pierre, who was one of the wealthiest merchants in Calais, stepped forward. "It is not right that our people should starve to death if any way can be found to prevent it," he said. "I shall go as the first of the six."

"And I will be the second," said John Daire, another wealthy merchant.

Two brothers, James and Peter Wisant, followed, then two more. A woman in the crowd started to weep, another called out a blessing. Coldly, without emotion, these men were giving their lives for their fellow citizens. The six men were dressed in sackcloth and rope halters were placed round their necks. Accompanied by weeping crowds, they walked barefooted to the gates of Calais, and then on, alone, into the English camp.

Coming into the King's presence, they fell on their knees, offering up the keys of the castle and the town and surrendering themselves to his mercy. The English nobles present were very impressed with the courage of the six men and begged the King to be merciful. But Edward was still angry and was determined that Calais should suffer for the damage done and the English lives which had been lost. He ordered the executioner to be sent for. Eustache de St Pierre and his companions realized that they had only a short time left to live.

A ripple passed through the crowd, heads turned, men backed away from the entrance and bowed. A woman stood in the doorway. For a moment she looked at the captives, then she moved slowly forward, the ample folds of her gown not quite concealing the fact that she was soon to have a child. It was Philippa the queen. She knelt at the King's feet and looked up at him. He saw that there were tears in her eyes.

"Gentle sir," she said, "since I have crossed the sea with great danger to see you I have never asked you for one favour. Now I most humbly ask, for the sake of the Son of the Blessed Mary and your love for me, that you will be merciful to these six men."

For a long moment the King looked at her in silence, then he sighed. "Lady, I wish you had been anywhere else but here. You have entreated in such a manner that I cannot refuse you. I therefore give them to you to do with as you please." –

Queen Philippa had the captives taken to her apartments, gave them food and clothing and sent them on their way with gifts of money. She had saved the six men from death, and her husband from an unworthy action. This was Philippa, "the most gentle queen, most liberal and most courteous that ever was in her days."

Assembly

Let us close our eyes and think. Let us think about getting our own back. King Edward wanted the citizens of Calais to suffer for the harm they had done him. He was not a particularly vengeful man, but this time he was determined to get his own back. Queen Philippa managed to make him change his mind.

There are times when we all feel we want to get our own back on people who have hurt us, and then it is difficult to be generous and forgiving, but if everyone tries to get his own back when will it stop? It will go on and on. Do we really want to live like that? Isn't it better, and more comfortable, to make the effort and stop, to forgive, and forget about getting our own back?

Classwork

Tell us about:　anyone you know who always likes to get his or her own back.

Discuss:　"Half the bloodshed in the world is caused by people wanting to get their own back."

Find out:　What is a vendetta? (They happened especially in Corsica, Sardinia and Sicily.)

Group improvisation:　Divide into groups of 8–10. The action takes place in a frontier town in the Wild West during the nineteenth century. The Boones and the Cassidys have been fighting each other for years. People have died on both sides, most recently a young man of the Boone family. The scene is set in the Boone family home, and you are all members of the Boone family. As usual, revenge is being planned, but this time at least one member of the family wants to end the feud. Show the scene where he or she tries to persuade the family to his or her way of thinking. End the scene as you think best.

Individual work:　*a.* Write a character sketch of "The most unforgiving person I know".

　　　　　　b. Find out all about modern Calais and write an advertisement brochure to attract holidaymakers to the town.

4

Androcles and the Lion

About two thousand years ago, when Rome was master of all the known world, there lived, in North Africa, a slave called Androcles whose Roman master was very unkind and often had him cruelly beaten. Finally, Androcles decided he could stand it no longer and, though he knew that if he was recaptured he would be either crucified or thrown to the wild animals in the arena, he ran away from his master.

He got safely away and kept going until he came to the edge of the desert. There he found a cave. Creeping thankfully into its shade, he threw himself down and fell asleep.

Sometime later he woke up. There was a strong animal smell in the cave. Slowly Androcles pulled himself up and cautiously moved towards the entrance. He didn't think there was anyone within miles of this deserted spot, but he wasn't taking any chances.

Suddenly a shadow moved, and a huge shape blocked out the sunshine—it was a fully grown lion! With growing horror, Androcles realized he had been sleeping in a lion's den, and now the lion had come home. Keeping as still as death, he watched the lion limp into the cool shade just inside the cave mouth and sink heavily to the ground. It turned a paw over and, growling softly, began to lick it. It was lame—perhaps there was a thorn in its foot.

Then the lion looked up, straight at Androcles. There was no escape and he was unarmed. Androcles' knees gave way and he slumped to the ground in terror, expecting any moment to feel those fearful teeth in his flesh.

But nothing happened. The lion looked at the man and Androcles stared, terror-stricken, at the beast. Time passed, then the lion dropped its head and licked its paw again. Amazed, Androcles realized the animal was in such pain it simply wasn't interested in the free meal offered by the slave's thin body.

Then Androcles did something extraordinary. Forgetting his own danger, he went up to the lion and gently took the sore paw between his hands—and the lion let him! It growled softly, as a warning, but quietened as Androcles spoke soothingly to it. Gently the slave examined the paw and found there was a large thorn embedded in the pad. Slowly, carefully, Androcles pulled out the thorn. The lion jerked its paw away. Its tongue rasped over the sore pad. Then it thrust its head towards Androcles and licked his face!

From then on, the man and the lion shared the same cave. The lion would go off hunting and bring back the best part of its kill for Androcles. He would take the meat and put it on a rock in the blazing mid-day sun, which was almost as good as cooking it.

They lived happily enough for three years, until Androcles, tiring of living an animal's life, decided to risk going back to the world of men. Surely, he thought, they'll have forgotten about me by now and I can live somewhere quietly. But they hadn't forgotten. He was recognized as a runaway slave by some Roman soldiers, arrested, and then sent back to his master, who had now returned to Rome. There Androcles was tried and sentenced to death.

The Romans were a cruel people who delighted in blood sports. They captured fierce animals, starved them until they became mad with hunger, then released them into the arena where the poor condemned prisoners waited. The resulting flow of blood was enough to satisfy even the Roman audience who sat watching in safety high above the arena.

When Androcles' turn came, he closed his eyes and waited for death. He could hear the roars of the hungry lion as it threw itself against the gate of its prison. Then the gate opened. The lion bounded out and stood blinking in the sunshine. The audience gasped in admiration. This was a huge beast. The lion saw Androcles and crouched for the spring. Its muscles tensed and it leaped towards the trembling figure. Androcles staggered—the audience gasped. The lion had rubbed its head against the man's legs. Now it was frisking around him like a puppy! With incredulous delight, Androcles realized that this was *his* lion and he flung his arms round the beast's neck.

The audience shouted its approval. The arena echoed with applause. Never had such a sight been seen before. When the people heard Androcles' story they demanded that he be granted his freedom and given the lion as a present. From then on Androcles and the lion lived happily together.

Assembly

Let us close our eyes and think. Let us think about being kind to animals. The ancient Romans were very cruel, but, even today, not everyone is kind to animals. The Royal Society for the Prevention of Cruelty to Animals is kept busy, not because people enjoy being cruel but because they are too lazy or too thoughtless to avoid cruelty.

Every year puppies and kittens are given as presents, especially at Christmas-time, and, every year, when the baby animals grow up, there are owners who turn them out to fend for themselves. Let us be sure that we and our friends realize that this means condemning the animals to a slow and painful death.

We have responsibilities towards those creatures less clever than ourselves. Let us always remember that animals were not put on earth just to amuse us.

Classwork

Tell us about: a. any partnership you know of between a human and an animal.

b. any case you have heard of involving cruelty to animals.

Discuss: a. "If British people gave all the money they spend on pet food to famine relief it would save many thousands of human lives."

b. We are exploring the universe. One day, we may meet a race far more intelligent than mankind. How they treat us may depend on how we have treated inferior forms of life on this planet.

Find out: Use the History section of the school library. Find a picture of a Roman amphitheatre, e.g. the Colosseum in Rome.

Group improvisation: Rabies is a dreadful disease which is on the increase in Europe and for which there is no sure cure. Animals carry rabies, so animals coming into Britain have to spend six months in quarantine until the health authorities are sure they are free of rabies.

Customs officials have discovered the Smiths' pet dog hidden on the boat after the family's return from France. The Smiths say the dog has not left the boat and anyway they cannot afford to pay for the dog to be kept in quarantine for six months.

They are told the only alternative is for the dog to be destroyed, which upsets the Smith children very much.

Divide into two groups; one is the Smith family, the other consists of customs officers and other travellers. Improvise the scene that takes place just after the discovery of the dog.

Individual work: Write a story or a play. Think how mankind uses animals for its own purposes. Now imagine that a race of superior beings conquers the earth and write in story or play form about how these beings might use humans.

5

The Birth of Bandoola

"Elephant Bill" or, to give him his correct name, Mr J. H. Williams, has written a number of books about the wonderfully intelligent animals he worked with in Burma. From all the hundreds of elephants he knew, one stands out supreme—the huge and magnificent tusker, Bandoola. But, if it hadn't been for his "auntie", Bandoola might never have grown up at all.

A human baby is only carried for nine months inside its mother, but it takes two years before a baby elephant is ready to be born. About a year before the birth, the mother elephant is adopted by another female elephant who is known as the "auntie". The auntie becomes the constant companion of the expectant mother. She helps her prepare for the birth, guards her during the birth and helps her look after the baby when it is born.

The trained elephants of Burma have a considerable amount of freedom. Bandoola's mother and auntie were owned by a contractor who hired out his elephants to a teak company. The elephants worked from early morning until mid-day dragging the huge tree trunks down to the river, then were allowed to roam free so that they could forage for food. They often wandered many miles from camp.

When the time approached for the birth, the two elephants made their way to a special place they had selected. It was a flat area at the bend of a river, protected on three sides by silently running water so that the slightest noise would warn the elephants of danger. In the centre of this "maternity ward" stood a huge tree which would give shade in the heat of the day, and all around grew seven-foot-high elephant grass which provided plentiful supplies of food.

The two animals spent most of the night stamping down the elephant grass in a wide area around the tree so that nothing could creep up on them without being seen. Then the mother moved towards the centre and the auntie circled round, keeping guard. Before long the baby elephant was born.

Not far away a tiger stretched himself. He had detected the smell of the new-born elephant calf and was hungry—elephant calf would be a rare delicacy. To get at the calf the tiger had first to stampede the auntie, then attack and drive off the mother so that the calf would be left unprotected. Surprise was essential; if the elephants were warned they would be far more difficult to frighten and stampede.

The tiger crept nearer. A superb hunter, he moved slowly and carefully until the great bulk of the auntie showed against the paler sky. Suddenly, with tremendous power, the tiger catapulted forward and landed on her back. His foreclaws and teeth dug into her shoulder. His razor-sharp back claws raked her sides.

The auntie trumpeted in pain. She flayed round with her trunk but couldn't reach the beast on her back. The only way to get rid of the monstrous, clawing thing was to scrape it off with the overhanging branch of a tree. In terror the elephant stampeded for the forest.

The tiger then slipped off her back and turned to Bandoola's mother. The little calf, wobbly and uncertain, was standing between his mother's forelegs. Gently her trunk pushed him further back. She lowered her head and waited. Her back was protected by the tree trunk so the tiger couldn't attack her rear. He veered to one side as her trunk came down like a whiplash. The tiger snarled. His paw struck with claws outstretched and the elephant shrieked in pain, her trunk hanging numb and useless. Then the beast leaped at her side, his hind claws slicing her flesh like butcher's knives. She screamed in rage and pain and tried to shake him off, but gradually she weakened.

Suddenly a thunderbolt charged across the clearing and flung itself against the mother's heaving flank. The auntie had returned and had squashed the tiger between her own body and that of her friend. With a roar of pain the tiger dropped to the ground and slunk quickly away, while the two elephants trumpeted defiance.

The noise they made brought men from the timber camp running with torches and spears. As they came closer they saw, peeping out from between his mother's great forefeet, the little piggy eyes and stubby trunk of the plump little baby elephant. During the whole of the fight he hadn't moved an inch. Then and there they decided to call him "Bandoola", after a great Burmese hero, for this elephant was obviously born to great things.

Assembly

Let us close our eyes and think. Let us think about friends. In times of trouble we all need a friend, just as Bandoola and his mother needed their auntie. We won't be called upon to face a tiger's attack for our friends, but sharp tongues can also hurt. It is as easy to panic and run away from scornful laughter as it is to run away from pain and terror.

Have we the courage to stand with our friends, even if it means being laughed at or made fun of? We expect our friends to be loyal to us. Let us think for a moment of how much loyalty we have to give them.

Classwork

Tell us about: a. a time when you were glad of your friend's support.

b. a time when someone you thought was your friend let you down.

Discuss: "In some ways it is easier to fight for your friend than to risk being laughed at."

Find out: what working conditions are like for elephants in the teak forests of Burma.

Group improvisation: Divide into groups of 6–8. Plan a scene which ends with one character saying to another, "To you a friend is just someone you can use. I've had enough—goodbye!"

Plan your play carefully before you start to rehearse. In this case, the final line is the climax (the most exciting point) of the play. You need at least one good reason for it to be said, probably more than one.

Individual work: Write a story about a friendship between two animals or between an animal and a human, preferably based on something you know to be true.

6

New Year's Eve (*Nos Galan*)

The people of Mountain Ash, a small town in South Wales, have a very special way of celebrating New Year's Eve [*Nos Galan* in Welsh], for this is the time when they honour the memory of a local hero who died more than 200 years ago and yet is still remembered with admiration and affection. His name was Griffith Morgan and he was born at Nythbran farm near Porth in the Rhondda Valley, just over the mountain from Mountain Ash. To all Welshmen he was known as Guto Nythbran [pronounced Gitoh Nithbrahn] and he was one of the greatest runners that ever lived.

There are dozens of stories about Guto. One of the stories tells how when he was a boy his mother found she had run out of sugar and casually asked her son to run down to the shop to get her some. Guto took her at her word, and he ran all the way to the nearest town to fetch the sugar and back again (about seven miles altogether) before his mother's kettle had boiled! As a young man he is said to have been so fast that he could catch a bird in flight.

Today Welshmen are Rugby fans, but in Guto's day they were running fans and gambled all they could afford, and sometimes more, on the outcome of a foot race.

Challengers came from far and wide to race Guto, usually over long distances and never on a proper race track—in the eighteenth century such things simply did not exist. Their kind of running was more like our cross-country races, but usually with only two runners taking part.

Guto was not very bright but he had a sweetheart, Sian, who was a keen business woman. She ran a shop as well as acting as Guto's manager.

Guto's fame spread far and wide as he beat opponent after opponent and, at last, there was no one left to challenge him. For years he lived a quiet life until, one day, a message came from the village of Bedwas, about fifteen miles away, to say they had a young man who was a prince of runners, good enough even to beat Guto.

The people of Mountain Ash were indignant. How could this so-called "Prince of Bedwas" think that he could beat their Guto? At once they set about persuading their hero to accept the challenge, but Guto was thirty-seven years old and had not run for years. The lad from Bedwas was much younger and was very fit indeed.

Did Guto hesitate? It's unlikely that he realized fully the risks involved. Anyway the challenge was accepted. The race arranged was to be from Newport, in Monmouthshire, to Bedwas church, a distance of twelve miles. Bets were laid, and large sums staked on the outcome. It would have been difficult for Guto to draw back even if he had wanted to. He would have been letting down his friends and, above all, his sweetheart. Sian was quite happily convinced that Guto would romp home.

Sian was right. Even out of condition Guto was in a class by himself, and he left the "Prince of Bedwas" far behind. Seeing Sian waiting for him at the finishing line, Guto put on a final spurt and crossed the line to the jubilant shouts of his supporters. Sian rushed forward to congratulate him giving him a hearty slap on the back—"Well done Guto bach!"

But the final sprint at the end of twelve gruelling miles had put a considerable strain on the runner's heart, and the heavy slap was the last straw. With a gasp, Guto collapsed at her feet—and died.

His grief-stricken friends carried Guto's body home and he was buried in a little churchyard at the top of the mountain between Porth and Mountain Ash.

On New Year's Eve, races are run through the streets of Mountain Ash in memory of Guto. At first there were only men's races but now there is also a race for women in honour of the courage of a modern runner, Lillian Board.

Men and women come from all over Britain to compete in the races. The climax comes about forty minutes before midnight when the waiting crowds see a rocket burst high above the mountain top and know that the "mystery runner", who symbolizes the spirit of Guto Nythbran, has set off from Guto's graveside to carry his blazing torch down the steep, four-mile-long road into Mountain Ash where he will light the New Year (Nos Galan) flame in the centre of the town. No one knows who the runner is until he appears, but it is always a famous athlete.

As the flame flares up the runners prepare themselves for the final four-mile race around the houses, which will bring in the New Year, and once more the great spirit of Guto Nythbran is honoured in the hills and valleys of South Wales.

Assembly

Let us close our eyes and think. Let us think about the way we use the gift of life. Guto's way was to run and never count the cost. Lillian Board's way was to face with courage everything that life brought, even when it was a painful, killing disease.

What is our way of life? Sometimes we grumble about such little things, we feel so sorry for ourselves that we forget to be grateful for the gift of life.

Guto and Lillian died when they both had so much to live for. *We* are *alive*. As we breathe the fresh air, as we run and laugh, let us be thankful we are *alive*!

Classwork

Tell us about: a time when you have run so hard you felt you could collapse.

Discuss: The motto of the Olympic Games is: "Swifter, higher, stronger." Could this be a suitable motto for life? or would you prefer this? "It's not the winning or the losing that counts, but how you run the race."

Find out: about Lillian Board. Who was she? What did she do? What was she like?

Group improvisation: Divide into groups of 8–10. The scene is set in a dressing-room after an important sporting event. One member of the team has not done as well as expected. One of his or her team mates suspects that there is an unworthy reason for this. The rest of the team vary in their opinions. Finish the episode as you think best.

Individual work: *a.* Prepare a three-minute talk on the life and career of an athlete you admire.

b. Write a story which begins, "The boy from Greenland looked at his schoolmates in amazement. 'What's all the fuss about?' he asked. 'After all, it's *only* a game! . . .' "

7

The Vicar and the Goat

Human beings are accustomed to thinking themselves a cut above the rest of creation. We look down on animals. We say, "Look at that chimp, it's nearly human," as if that is the greatest compliment we could possibly pay. But, you know, in some ways animals are superior to humans. We all know that elephants are stronger, hawks can see further and most animals can use their noses better than we can. But sometimes animals even have better temperaments than we have.

Have you ever been unkind to your dog, spoken harshly to it, perhaps even hit it? Yet, the moment you get over your bad temper, your pet will come running up, all ready to forgive and forget. There aren't many humans who are as forgiving as that.

Perhaps it needs a very special kind of man to really learn a lesson from an animal. Some time ago there lived just such a man, a vicar in the small market town of Llandovery, in Wales. He lived there until he was an old man, greatly respected by everyone who knew him.

Mr Pritchard, the vicar, was a saintly man and, because people were fond of him, they talked about him. Soon a whole series of stories grew up round his name. Whether they were all absolutely true I don't know, but they all reflected the affection everyone felt for him.

One of these stories tells of a time when the young Mr Pritchard wasn't at all saintly. In fact, he was a bit of a waster, spending far too much time and money on drinking. Every evening he would stroll down to the local public house and stay there until closing time when he would stagger home thoroughly drunk.

Mr Pritchard didn't have a dog, but he had a pet goat of whom he was very fond. The goat accompanied its master every night to the public house. It would wait patiently while he drank his fill, then trot primly home beside its master.

One evening, young Mr Pritchard suddenly thought what a very selfish man he was. Here he was enjoying the best beer, and there was his poor goat with a mouth as dry as dust. Anxious to make amends and share his pleasure with his pet he called for a bowl, and, filling it up with beer, set it down in front of the goat. After an exploratory sniff the animal sank its beard in the bowl and lapped eagerly. Pleased, Mr Pritchard called for the bowl to be refilled, and the goat drank it dry. Again and again the man refilled his tankard, and the goat had its bowlful until, by the light of the moon, two figures could be seen, one on two legs and one on four, lurching homeward down the lane.

They had shared the night's entertainment and, next morning, they shared something else—an almighty headache! However, by the evening they had both recovered and set out together for the pub.

Arriving there Mr Pritchard called for a tankard for himself and a bowlful of beer for his goat. When they were filled, he set down the bowl on the floor and picked up his tankard. "Your health," he cried. The goat looked at him, then at the bowl of beer. With an expression of utter disgust on its face, it turned its back and walked away. Once was enough for any self-respecting goat!

Mr Pritchard looked at his tankard and then at his goat. He took a deep breath. "If a goat has the sense to say, 'Stop, that's enough!' surely so must a man. I'll never touch another drop," he said. And he never did.

It takes a really great man to be humble enough to learn from a goat.

Assembly

Let us close our eyes and think. Let us think about learning from animals. Are human beings conceited? We are, after all, only rather a superior kind of animal ourselves. We may be more intelligent than any other animal, but does that give us the right to be proud and look down on all other animals?

Is there anything we can learn from animals? Our pets for instance, can they teach us anything?—perhaps tolerance, or patience, or forgiveness?

Classwork

Tell us about: a. a time when you have watched and admired something an animal was doing.

b. anyone you have read about or heard of who has learned something from an animal or bird.

Discuss: a. "A dog is a man's best friend."

b. "Man is the only animal that kills for reasons other than food."

Find out: as much as you can about the R.S.P.C.A. (Royal Society for the Prevention of Cruelty to Animals). How does it work in your area? Are there any other groups of people who work for animal welfare?

Group improvisation: Divide into groups of 6–8. Farmer Jones has suffered considerable loss from the raids of foxes on his chicken runs. He comes home determined to exterminate the vermin by poison, shooting, or inviting the local hunt on to his land. His children are very upset because they have taken a great interest in one family of foxes and have watched the cubs grow up.

With father and children at loggerheads, mother tries to be peacemaker. Work out the scene and resolve the problem as you think best.

Individual work: Write a story about a prisoner who has a great loathing for a certain kind of animal or insect. One day he discovers one of these in his cell. At first horrified, he gradually comes to admire the little creature.

8

The Black Death at Eyam

Most of you have probably, at one time or another, helped to amuse young brothers or sisters by playing that old nursery game, "Ring a ring of roses". Small children seem to love it, especially the bit where they make big brother sit down bump on the floor! Few people now realize what that rhyme actually means. It originated 300 years ago, at the time of the Great Plague.

"Ring a ring of roses"—the roses were the rash of red, plague spots on the victim's skin.

"A pocket full of posies"—people carried posies, or bunches of sweet-smelling herbs, to hold to their noses in the hope of avoiding the nasty smells which they thought carried the plague.

"Atishoo, atishoo,"—sneezing was one of the first symptoms, for plague affected the lungs, and sneezes and coughs spread the germs over everyone near.

"We all fall down,"—dead! There was no known cure for the plague.

After the time of the Crusades, England was ravaged by the dreaded plague known as the Black Death. In London, during the month of August, 1665, 17,000 people died of the plague. In September, there were 31,000 deaths. It was as if every third person in the town suddenly died. People fled from the Black Death as they would from a tidal wave. They hoped to save themselves in the clean air of the countryside. But, all too often, they carried the plague with them, and thousands more died as a result in villages and towns throughout the country.

When the plague was at its height, in September 1665, someone noticed that one of the victims owned a large wardrobe of fashionable clothes. Thinking it a pity to waste so much finery, that person packed the clothes in a box and sold it. Eventually the box arrived at a tailor's shop in Eyam, a small village on the edge of the Derbyshire moors. A few days later that tailor was dead.

Across the road from the tailor's home was the grey stone cottage where a young girl called Emmot Sydall lived with her father, brother and four sisters. Every day Emmot slipped out of Eyam to a little, wooded valley with a stream bubbling through.

There she met Rowland Torre from the next village. Together they made plans for their future, for they were soon to marry.

Then the plague came to Eyam and something quite extraordinary happened, something which happened nowhere else. The rector, William Mompesson, and his wife Catherine, together with the Puritan minister Thomas Stanley, persuaded the villagers not to run away but to isolate themselves at Eyam until the plague had burned itself out. If they ran away they might save *themselves*, but they ran the risk of taking the plague to everyone they met.

The villagers of Eyam decided to stay and risk their *own* lives rather than pass on the plague. They isolated themselves completely from the outside world. No one entered or left the village. No message or letter was sent out—except one, from the rector to the Lord Lieutenant of the county, asking him to arrange for food to be left in a lonely place beside a well outside the village. In payment, money would be put into a pitcher which would be lowered into the well. Vinegar would then be poured into the well to purify the water and cleanse the coins so that they could be taken up in safety by the tradesmen who supplied the food.

Secretly one contact was kept up for a while. Occasionally, Emmot was able to get away to meet Rowland. He begged her to come away to safety with him, but Emmot said she loved him too much to bring him the plague as her dowry. By the end of October, twenty-nine people were dead, including Emmot's father, brother and four sisters. She told Rowland it was too dangerous to go on meeting and she would not see him again until the plague was over. He begged and pleaded with her, but sorrowfully Emmot left him and went back to Eyam.

For six months the villagers of Eyam remained isolated, seeing their families and friends sicken and die. Sometimes the number of deaths lessened, and those who were left began to hope that it was over. Then the plague would break out again, and they knew their ordeal must go on. The strain must have been almost intolerable. No one knew whose turn it would be next. However strong and healthy you were, in a few days you might be dead and buried.

The old nursery rhyme draws the picture very clearly—"We all fall down". Out of the 300 people who lived in Eyam at the start of their isolation, only thirty-three remained alive when the plague was over.

One of the first people into the village when the church bell rang out the news of the end of the isolation was Rowland Torre—but his Emmot was dead.

The self-sacrifice of the people of Eyam was not wasted. The plague was contained and the people of the surrounding villages were spared.

Assembly

Let us close our eyes and think. Let us think about being considerate towards other people. 300 years ago, the simple villagers of Eyam gave their lives rather than pass on the Black Death to their neighbours. We haven't to face their dreadful decision but, from time to time, we are given something nasty which we can either keep to ourselves or pass on. It may be only a cold or a bit of gossip, but our sneezes splashed over the frail and the elderly can give them bronchitis which can sometimes be very serious, and what seems only a bit of gossip to us can often cause someone pain and heartache.

How many times have you known someone to be hurt by a bit of gossip? Have you ever thought that passing on gossip is as bad as passing on poison? Think about it now.

Classwork

Tell us about: a. any time when you have been hurt by gossip.

b. any time you know when germs have been passed on by someone who was not sufficiently careful.

Discuss: a. "Passing on gossip is as bad as passing on poison." Is this true?

b. Working hours lost through colds, coughs and 'flu cost us valuable production time. If we could eliminate these diseases it would go a long way towards improving the living standards of everyone in this country.

Find out: What was the Black Death? How was it passed on? Does this disease ever occur today?

Group improvisation: "Coughs and sneezes spread diseases" was one of the favourite slogans of the Second World War. Imagine you are a group of actors travelling from factory to factory performing sketches in the works' canteens to drive this message home. Show the class one of the sketches.

Individual work: Prepare a campaign to educate the public in preventing the spread of diseases. Think of as many aspects of preventive medicine and hygiene as you can. You can use any means to get your message across (posters, slogans, T.V. and radio commercials, etc.).

9

Philemon and Baucis

The people of ancient Rome believed in many gods. They called the king of the gods Jupiter, and told many stories of the wonderful deeds he was supposed to have performed. This is one of the stories.

Jupiter was in the habit of making periodic visits to different parts of the earth to check up on the behaviour of humans. One day he asked his messenger and fellow god, Mercury, to accompany him on a visit to the land of Phrygia. They didn't go in the splendour and glory of gods but dressed as ordinary travellers.

When they arrived, looking tired and footsore, they knocked on the door of the nearest house and asked if they might rest there.

"Certainly not," replied the owner. "Be off with you!"

Jupiter hid his annoyance and they went on to the next house. But there too they were turned away, and at the next house and the next. Each householder seemed to be more unpleasant than the last. Nowhere could they find rest or even a drink to refresh them in the heat of the day.

Jupiter was angry. "Is there no one in this country who is kind enough to offer us hospitality?" he cried.

"Look," said Mercury pointing to a tiny thatched cottage high on the hillside. "We haven't tried there."

Wearily the two gods climbed the hill. As they approached the cottage the door opened and an old man appeared. He stopped short as he saw them, then hurried forward. "Good sirs," he said, "you look very tired. Won't you come inside and rest in the shade?"

Gratefully they entered the cottage and sat down while the old man, whose name was Philemon, brought out a pitcher of wine and some mugs.

"Have you travelled far, gentlemen?" he asked.

"Far enough to be glad of a rest." Jupiter took the mug gratefully.

"Are you hungry? Would you like something to eat?" Philemon asked. "My wife, Baucis, would be glad to get you a meal."

The travellers thanked him and sipped their wine as Baucis bustled around preparing a meal of simple, country fare: home-cured bacon, vegetables from the garden, and fruit and nuts.

C

When all was ready, Philemon turned to his guests. "Please come and eat," he said. "We wish we could provide you with better fare, but this is all we have. We are poor people."

The gods smiled and thanked him, then they sat down to tuck into their meal with a hearty appetite. Philemon stretched out his hand for the empty pitcher. He hoped there was enough wine in the barrel to refill it. To his amazement, far from being empty the pitcher was overflowing with wine.

"May I have some more?" Mercury held out his mug. Philemon hastened to re-fill it, then looked into the jug. It was full again.

The old man gazed from his guests to the pitcher. However much they drank, the pitcher remained full. Realizing these were no ordinary men, he shrank back in fear.

Jupiter smiled. "*You* have nothing to fear," he said. "But I must punish everyone else in this country for their selfishness and lack of kindness. Come, follow us to the top of the mountain."

Trembling, Philemon and Baucis obeyed. As they climbed behind the two gods, they glanced back into the valley below and saw the water of the river rise and flood the countryside until all the houses were covered except their little cottage. Suddenly, as they gazed, their cottage was transformed into a beautiful, shining temple.

Jupiter turned to the old couple. "Name anything you desire and it shall be given you."

Philemon and Baucis looked at each other. They didn't want riches or power. They were perfectly happy as they were, so what could they ask for? Suddenly Philemon smiled. "If it please you, lord," he said, "my wife and I would like to live here peacefully together serving you in the temple. Then, when the time comes for us to die, we would like to die both together at the same moment. We both dread the thought of being the one left alive and alone. The loneliness would be more than either of us could bear."

Their wish was granted. Philemon and Baucis lived together in peaceful old age until, suddenly, one day, they died, both at the same moment, and were transformed into two trees, an oak and a lime, which grew side by side on the mountain.

Assembly

Let us close our eyes and think. Let us think of old people we know who live alone. Few old couples are as fortunate as Philemon and Baucis. However much they may wish to die "both at the same moment", it usually happens that one partner is left alone, desolate and lonely, without the companion of a lifetime.

There is not much we can do to comfort such a loss but we can try to make life a little less lonely for the one left behind. All we need to give is our time—time to listen and be interested while the lonely one talks.

Are we so full of our own concerns that we have no time to give to those who are old and alone? Is there no one in our neighbourhood who would be glad of a short visit every now and then? Let us spend a quiet moment thinking. Is there someone? Can we help?

Classwork

Tell us about: any person you know, or have heard of, who is lonely.
Discuss: "Old people are not all pallid, pathetic and poor," said a social worker. What did he mean? Why did he think it was necessary to say so?
Find out: *a.* What is hypothermia? How can it be prevented?
   b. How many Old People's Homes are there in your area? Are the residents able to be independent, or are all their needs catered for by professional workers?
Group improvisation: Divide into groups of about 6. A family group are discussing the problem of the Grandfather. He lives alone but is finding it increasingly difficult to cope for himself. The question is, does he go into some sort of a Home or does he come to live with the family? Mother, father and each of the children have their own points of view and hold to them strongly.

The discussion is at its height when Grandfather walks in. Finish the scene as you think best.
Individual work: *a.* Write a description of what you consider would be an ideal home for old people, either communal or individual, whichever you think best. Would you like to live there when you are old?
   b. Draw and describe a simple aid of your own design which will help old people in some way (e.g. a way of alerting the neighbours in case of accident).

Hereward and the Witch

1066—everyone knows that date. Everyone knows that in that year William, Duke of Normandy, defeated King Harold at the Battle of Hastings. But not many people know that three years after the battle William still hadn't got control of all his new kingdom.

There were some excellent leaders of rebel groups who organized hit-and-run raids on the Normans. The most famous of these was Hereward the Wake. Eventually William succeeded in cornering Hereward on the Isle of Ely. Ely is built on a hill and was, in those days, entirely surrounded by marshes which were far too dangerous to cross unless you knew the way, and, of course, the Normans didn't. The only way William could hope to get his men across was by the Aldreth causeway, a raised pathway through the marshes. Hereward knew this and took care to see that it was always well guarded.

William tried everything he could think of, but Hereward countered every attack. Nothing the King could do succeeded. The whole might of the Norman army was put to scorn by a handful of English fighters. It must have seemed to the Normans as if some special power was fighting against them.

In those days everyone believed in magic and the power of witches and, if you believe in that power, it becomes a very real thing. William's friends suggested he should use magic to defeat Hereward. At first William refused, but at last he agreed to seek the help of a witch who lived nearby. Perhaps he thought Hereward had already been using magic against him. Hereward seemed to have foreknowledge of so many of William's plans.

In fact Hereward did have foreknowledge, but not through witchcraft. He was a very brave, clever man, and he used his intelligence to fight his far stronger enemy. Hereward had the local fen men teach him the way to get across the marshes. It was dangerous but not impossible. Sometimes they had to use leaping poles to propel themselves across the most treacherous parts. Before setting out, Hereward would disguise himself so that, when he reached the other side, he could mingle with the Normans without arousing suspicion. In this way he had been able to overhear a number of William's plans.

On one occasion, he disguised himself as a poor Saxon potter and made his way into the Norman stronghold, where he found a night's lodging in the house of a woman who happened to be a friend of the very witch William had decided to employ.

During the night Hereward heard someone moving. The witch had come to visit her friend, and the two women were quietly leaving the house. Hereward was curious. He followed them to a nearby spring which was reputed to be the abode of an evil spirit, and hid himself nearby. The two women didn't bother to lower their voices. Since they spoke to each other in Norman French and addressed the spirit in Latin, they thought no one would understand what they said, certainly not the illiterate Saxon potter who they thought was asleep in the house. Hereward, of course, did understand and listened in fascination as the witch called upon the evil spirit to help her during the next Norman attack on the causeway. She would stand on the top of a high wooden tower where everyone could see her and hurl down curses on the defenders, who would be so terrified that the Normans would cut through them like a knife through butter.

Hereward thought that the plan might well work, so next morning he wasted no time in getting back to Ely and making preparations for the coming attack.

The attack began when the Normans poured on to the end of the causeway. As soon as the English came out to defend it the witch, on the top of her tower, raised her arms and, in a weird and terrifying voice, began her magic incantations. Nervously the English looked at her. Hereward signalled the men he had stationed ready with blazing torches, and at once they set fire to the reeds which grew everywhere around. The strong wind fanned the flames, and a line of fire a quarter of a mile wide swept quickly towards the Normans. The roar of the flames and the crackling of the brushwood and willows made a terrible noise. The Norman soldiers ran for their lives. Many slipped into the bog and were drowned. Few of the rest escaped the arrows of the fen men who had crept out by secret ways to attack them. In the panic, the witch fell head-first from the tower and broke her neck. William himself was lucky to escape death in the confusion, and he never again tried to use magic to gain his ends.

Assembly

Let us close our eyes and think. Let us think about superstition. A lot of people even today try to use magic to get what they want, though they do not call it magic. How many of you take a lucky charm or mascot into an exam with you? Many people read their horoscopes in magazines and newspapers. Fortune-tellers make quite a lot of money at fairs and at the seaside.

We laugh at people who believe in magic potions, but lucky charms are just as silly. Isn't it all a little absurd, and wouldn't it be more sensible to rely on hard work a little more and "luck" a little less? Hereward used his intelligence to outwit William and his strength to defeat him. William tried to get special favours granted him by magic. Which way are we going to use—Hereward's, or William's?

Classwork

Tell us about: anyone you know who believes in horoscopes or fortune-telling.

Discuss: "There is no such thing as luck; it is just a question of taking every opportunity when it offers."

Find out: the derivation of the following superstitions:

  a. Touch wood.

  b. Four-leafed clovers bring good luck.

  c The number 13 brings bad luck.

Group improvisation: Divide into groups of 6–8. The scene is set inside a fortune-teller's tent. *This* fortune-teller is a fraud who tricks money out what she says. Think of ways in which she might do this and show how she sets about it.

Individual work: *a.* Prepare on tape a radio programme on superstition. If a tape recorder is not available, write a script for the programme. In the programme, you interview different people in order to get information about their superstitions. Try to find out about the superstitions of people in various professions, e.g. nurses, actors, farm workers, etc. Find out if there are different beliefs in different regions or countries.

  b. Write a story called, "Is it magic?"

The Hero and the "Drip"

When the Second World War broke out in 1939, Ted and Mary Jane lived next door to each other in a street exactly the same as all the other streets which were built in rows, one above the other, along a narrow, steep-sided valley. Down the middle of the valley ran a river, black with coal dust and steaming from the power station. A railway line ran beside the river, but there wasn't room down there for the road. That had been built about fifty feet higher up. At one point the road crossed from one side of the valley to the other on a wide bridge which spanned both the railway line and the river. Ted used to cross the bridge on his way to work every day.

During the war, all people over eighteen were "called up" to join the armed forces and fight for their country. When Ted was eighteen he had to go before the Medical Board so that the doctors could examine him and grade him. Strong, healthy men were graded "A1", and went into a combat unit. Anyone graded "C3" was considered unfit for the forces. Ted was C3. He was skinny and pasty-faced with spots. He worked as a clerk in the Town Hall and went home to dinner every day because the canteen food didn't suit him. He said his mother "understood his delicate stomach".

Mary Jane turned up her eleven-year-old nose. "What a drip," she thought, and sighed romantically over the soldiers dressed in hospital-blue who were home on convalescent leave after being injured in battle. These were *real* heroes, wounded soldiers, who were brave like soldiers in comics. Only drips stayed at home!

The valley was peaceful and quiet until, one day, the enemy bomber planes came looking for an oil refinery which was thirty miles away. Fighter planes attacked them and drove them off—all except one, which flew round in a wide circle hoping to come at the refinery from the rear. It was spotted and chased by a Spitfire. Realizing he had no hope of reaching his target, and slowed down by his heavy load, the Nazi pilot decided to get rid of his bombs and make for home as fast as possible.

It was about half-past one, and people in the valley were going back to work after lunch. All the bombs fell in a line down the valley. One narrowly missed the power station, a couple fell in the river, and two hit the railway line. One fell on a siding just above the bridge where a steam locomotive was shunting some coal trucks down to the main line. The coal trucks were blown to smithereens, and the engine was hurled on to the bank where it lay on its side, its steel plates buckled and steam screaming out of its damaged boiler.

Ted was on his way back to work and was just crossing the bridge over the railway line when he heard the roar of aeroplane engines and glanced up to see a large plane racing low down the valley towards him. Someone yelled "It's a German!" and he caught a glimpse of the black crosses on the wings as he dived for the foot of the nearest wall. There was a roar, the bridge shuddered and he coughed in the dust. Then the noise died down, except for the sound of the last bits of glass falling and the scream of steam escaping under pressure from the ruptured boiler—and, higher-pitched even than the steam, something else—which went on and on and abruptly stopped—the scream of the engine driver trapped in his cab in the path of that terrible steam.

There were a number of people about, but, before they could pull themselves together, a figure ran to the far end of the bridge, jumped the wall, threw himself down the steep, fifty-foot-high embankment and ran straight into the scalding steam which was still screaming out of the damaged engine. It was Ted, the drip!

The driver was trapped by his legs. It wasn't easy to free him, but Ted managed it and pulled the unconscious man out of the scalding steam. The driver was badly burned, but he lived. Ted had saved his life.

Both men were taken to hospital. The bomb-damage was cleared up, and that was the end of that incident—but not for Mary Jane. She wanted to see Ted. He was a hero now, and she felt he must be completely changed. She listened to her parents talking when her father came back from visiting Ted in hospital. "There's lots of bandages and he is covered with that violet stuff they put on burns, but he's not bad considering what he went through."

"Can he talk?"

"Oh yes, he asked his mother to bring him some milk jelly . . ."

Milk jelly! Mary Jane was disgusted. Heroes didn't ask for milk jelly. Anyway it was wartime and there was a shortage of food. Only a drip would fuss about his food in wartime. Mary Jane decided Ted was still a drip. But he was also a real, genuine hero and how could he be both at the same time? Mary Jane found it very puzzling. It took her a long time to realize that people are not always *only* what they seem to be.

Assembly

Let us close our eyes and think. Let us think how appearances can be mis-
leading. Think of an iceberg. We see the part that sticks up out of the
water, but four times as much of the iceberg is underneath the water
where we can't see it.

People are like icebergs—there is a great deal more to every human
being than we ever suspect from looking at the surface. Sometimes it
takes an extraordinary happening to show us what was there all the time,
so it is never wise to pin labels on a person and call him or her "a drip"
or "a weed" or "a square" or anything else. Think of someone you have
felt scornful about. Mary Jane felt very scornful of Ted. She was wrong.
You may be wrong too.

Classwork

Tell us about: anyone you know whose appearance or voice gives a
wrong idea of what they are really like.

Discuss: "All that glisters is not gold". What does Shakespeare mean
by this?

Find out: Read the casket scenes in Act 2, scenes 1 and 7 of *The Merchant of Venice* by William Shakespeare.

Group improvisation: In *The Merchant of Venice*, Shakespeare tells
how a wealthy man tried to make sure that, after his death, his daughter
would marry a wise man not a foolish one. Each of her suitors had to
choose between three caskets: one made of gold, one of silver and one of
lead. The successful man refused to be impressed by outward appearance
and chose the lead casket.

No modern father could set such a test but he would still want to be
sure his daughter did not marry a foolish man. Think about how he might
do it.

Divide into groups of 3. Two of you are the parents, the other is the
man who wants to marry your daughter. Take a few minutes to think
about it, the parents can discuss it together, then improvise the scene
where the parents try to satisfy themselves (in a subtle way) that the man
is sensible.

Individual work: a. Think of all the labels pinned on young people,
most of them uncomplimentary. Write a story showing how unfair it
can be to think that all young people are alike.

b. Lots of people think that male ballet dancers are
"cissy". Write an article for your school magazine proving what a false
idea this is.

Messer Ansaldo and his Cats

The old rhyme tells us that:
"In fourteen hundred and ninety two
Columbus sailed the ocean blue."
But it doesn't tell us if anyone sailed to America after him. In fact many people did so, for there were rich profits to be made by trading with the New World, if you could stand the dangers and hardships necessary to get there.

Early in the sixteenth century a rich merchant called Ansaldo degli Ormanni lived in Florence, a large city in Italy. He sailed three times to the New World and traded his goods for a considerable profit. The fourth time he set out, a furious tempest arose and blew his ship many miles off course. At last the storm blew itself out, and they sailed into a harbour on one of a group of islands which were quite unknown in those days, though we now call them the Canary Islands.

The king of the islands was very excited when he heard that a vessel had arrived. He hastened to greet the travellers and took them all to the palace for a royal banquet. Ansaldo was most impressed by the riches of the palace, but he was very puzzled by the strong young men who waited on the king, each of whom carried a great, long stick in his hand and stood behind the king's chair at the table.

The merchant soon realized why they were there. No sooner had the cooks started to bring in delicious-smelling dishes of food than there was a scampering and a squeaking, and a hoard of mice descended on the tables from all directions. The long sticks flew down right and left of the dish of food Ansaldo was sharing with the king, thus keeping the mice at bay. The other guests had to fend for themselves as best they could.

By signs the king explained that the whole island was overrun with the vermin and no one had discovered a way of destroying them. Ansaldo smiled and, jumping up, made signs to the king that he would soon return with a gift which would cure the plague of mice. He ran down to his ship and caught two of the ship's cats, strong, fine-looking animals, one male and one female, which he

carried swiftly back to the palace. Arriving there he asked that food
should be brought out again. Immediately the food arrived, so did
the hoards of mice. The two cats could hardly believe their good
fortune. They leapt from Ansaldo's arms and in a few minutes they
created such havoc among the mice that the survivors ran for their
lives.

The king was delighted with Ansaldo's gift and couldn't do
enough to show his gratitude. The merchant returned home with so
much gold, silver, pearls and jewels that he felt he could happily
retire and never work again.

On returning to Italy, Messer Ansaldo told many of his friends
about his good fortune in the distant islands. One of those who
listened hardest was called Giocondo de Fisanti. Giocondo decided
that he would go to the islands and try his fortune there too.
"After all," he reasoned, "if the king gave Ansaldo all those riches
just for a pair of cats, he will give *far* more to someone who presents
him with a really fine gift." So he sold all the land he possessed and,
with the money, bought jewels, fine rings and other precious gifts.

In case one of his friends should try to stop him, Giocondo
pretended he was setting out for the Holy Land. But, as soon as he
was out of sight, he set course for the island where the king had
his palace. Arriving there he was kindly greeted by the king, and
straight away Giocondo presented his rich gifts. The king was most
impressed, and decided he must give Giocondo a really valuable
present in return. So he sent for his most treasured possessions, and,
from the litter of kittens born to Ansaldo's cats, he chose the
finest kitten and presented it to Giocondo.

The Italian was furious. He thought the king was making fun of
him, but there was nothing he could do about it. So he stormed off,
cursing the king, the mice, and Messer Ansaldo and his cats. He
arrived back in Florence a much poorer man than when he set out.

But Giocondo was wrong to think that the king meant to make
fun of him. The king really had given him something he prized far
more highly than gold, silver or precious stones. The king's
intention was kindly; Giocondo's was not. He was simply hoping
to profit by the king's generosity and, in the event, was well
punished for his greed.

Assembly

Let us close our eyes and think. Let us think about giving and receiving, and about the true worth of a present. When we *give* a present do we give it freely, without hope of return, as Ansaldo did? Or do we give it merely to get back something better as Giocondo hoped to do?

When we are *given* a present, do we think, "How much is it worth?" or "How much time, effort and thought did it cost the giver?" Sometimes the biggest present, bought in the most expensive shop, is really worth far less than a tiny gift made by the giver's own hands.

Classwork

Tell us about: a time when you received a present you really did not want. Why do you think it was given to you?

Discuss: "There is a bit of the gold-digger in all of us!"

Find out: Read the story of the widow's mite in the New Testament (Luke, chapter 21).

Group improvisation: Divide into groups of 6–8. Think of a situation where a present has been given with the most kindly intentions, but which turns out unfortunately.

Talk about it in your group. Pool your ideas and decide which ideas to use. Then plan your play so that it works up to an exciting climax just before the end. Rehearse your play then show it to the rest of the class.

Individual work: a. Members of certain religious sects give a fixed percentage of their weekly income (sometimes as much as 20%) to their church so that it can be used for the common good. Write an essay giving the arguments for and against this policy.

b. Christ said that a poor widow's tiny gift was worth more than the rich presents of wealthy men. Write a story, set in modern times, to illustrate the same theme.

13

The Teenagers and the Seven-year-old

A coalmine has many miles of underground galleries branching out from the pit bottom but, of course, if you go to a coal-mining district, you won't expect to see any sign of these on the surface. What you may see are miles and miles of overhead wires running in all directions, which carry electricity to all parts of the mine, including the far-spreading underground galleries.

From the power station, the wire is carried safely overhead to the point where it has to be taken underground. Here it disappears inside "terminal towers". These are tall, square buildings, with plain, brick walls, about as high as a house but much smaller around. Each tower has an opening high up near the roof to let in the wires, which go through transformer switches in a little room at the top of the tower, and then into very heavily insulated cables which can be taken outside and into the ground.

The only way into this room is through a little hole in the floor from which a steep ladder leads down inside the tower to the ground. The only way into the tower is through a heavy wooden door which is always kept locked and barred.

One day workmen drove out from a coalmine to make alterations to a tower which was situated on land owned by the Coal Board, in a lonely spot some distance away from any paths or right of way used by the public. It had been decided to run an insulated cable through the tower at ground level, which was not to be connected in any way to the cable overhead. The workmen spent the day making a hole at ground level for the cable to enter on one side of the tower, and another on the opposite side for it to leave the tower.

When they finished work for the day, they covered both holes on the inside of the tower with very heavy metal sheets, and propped them in place with piles of bricks. Then they left, padlocking the door securely behind them. No one, they thought, could possibly get in, even if he risked trespassing on Coal Board land and ignored the large "danger" notices all round.

Later that evening, a group of teenage boys did trespass on the land, and, coming to the tower, noticed the small, newly-made holes. Together they pushed in the heavy metal plates, dislodging the piles of bricks inside the tower. Dropping to their knees, they peered inside the small holes. Seeing nothing of interest, they decided they'd had what fun they could, and went away.

After them came a little, seven-year-old boy. He was far too young to enter into their games, but old enough to be curious and follow them to see what they were doing. He found the little hole at the foot of the tower, too small for a teenager to enter but just the right size for a seven-year-old. Once inside, in the dim light, he must have seen the ladder leading up to the hole high above his head. Little boys are curious, so up he went towards the tiny room where three thousand volts of electricity sizzled across the wires.

No one knows quite what happened then. We only know that somehow the child crawled out of the tower and was found, sobbing pitifully, outside. His hands were horribly burned where the electricity had entered his body and his feet were burned where it had left. He must have been thrown from the ladder by the shock. Shortly afterwards he died in hospital.

It was a terrible accident—or was it an accident? The child could not have got into the tower if the teenagers had not pushed in the heavy metal sheets which covered the holes. They were far too heavy for the little boy to move. The teenagers would say it was the child's fault for going into the tower, and so it was. But has a seven-year-old got the same sense as a teenager? The most terrible thing about it was that it need not have happened. "Danger" and "No Trespassing" notices are not put up for fun. Danger means what it says. The teenagers knew this, but were quite confident that nothing would happen to *them*. They were old enough to look after themselves! True, they were, but a little thought and good sense on their part would have saved that child's life.

Assembly

Let us close our eyes and think. Let us think how something that seems, at the time, to be harmless fun can have tragic consequences. No one would deliberately condemn a child of seven to a painful death, yet the thoughtless fooling of a group of teenagers led to that result.

Let us think what we would feel like if our so-called "harmless" fun caused someone's death. Think—if a telephone kiosk is vandalized it can mean that it is not possible to get a doctor in time, and someone dies who need not have died. *This has happened.*

How many other times has stupid fooling about caused pain and suffering? Do we want this to happen because of us?

Classwork

Tell us about: a time when a game had unfortunate consequences for you or your friends (possibly a broken window or someone hit by a hard ball).

Discuss: How can we cure the vandal who says, "I did it for kicks"?

Find out: from your local council how much money has to be spent on repairing damage cause by vandals in your area.

Group improvisation: Divide into groups of about 6–8. (This is based on a recent case.) Billy and his friend have been playing on and around a bridge over a railway line. They have dropped a large coping-stone over the bridge on to a passing train. They saw it go through the roof of the luggage van, but do not know that it killed the guard. The boys, who are about twelve years old, return to Billy's home where the family are about to spend a normal evening. Then a policeman arrives to tell Billy's father what has happened.

Start your scene just before the policeman's arrival and show the reactions of the family to the news.

Individual work: a. Make a collection of newspaper-cuttings on cases of vandalism, especially any that could cause injury or death.

b. You are a scientific observer sent from another planet to study Earth's inhabitants. Your special assignment is a certain Post Office telephone kiosk at the corner of a street. You must record and describe everyone who enters it, adding your own comments and putting forward your own theories about what they are doing.

14

The Women of Fishguard

During the last war, we all thought Hitler would invade Britain. 200 years ago, everyone thought Napoleon Bonaparte would invade this country.

Britain was at war with France in 1797, but few thoughts of war had reached Pembrokeshire, the most western part of South Wales. Wednesday, 22 February, was a fine spring day, and the sea was unusually calm as Mr Thomas Williams, a retired sailor, took his morning stroll along the coast. He noticed four fine battleships, flying the British flag and crammed with troops. "Off to fight Johnny Frenchman," he thought proudly, as he lifted his telescope to his eye. To his horror he saw that the troops crammed together on the decks were *not* wearing British uniforms. These were French ships flying British flags to deceive the coastguard and carrying an invasion force which was about to land on a part of the coast which was totally unprepared to meet them. All preparations against invaders had been made on the south and east coasts of England. No one ever imagined the French would sail right round Land's End to a remote area of the Welsh coast.

Mr Williams sent a messenger galloping to the town of St David's, then followed the coast path northwards, keeping the ships in sight. At 4 p.m. they anchored off a rocky promontory, just out of sight of the thriving port of Fishguard. Here the commander of the French decided his troops should land.

The commander of the invasion force was General William Tate, an Irish American whose family had been killed by Indians in the American War of Independence. Because the Indians were on the British side, Tate had come to hate the British. The French were glad to use him in what was originally intended to be one of several raids against the British. He was given 1,200 men, mostly convicts, and enough guns and ammunition to arm the British peasants who were thought to be ready to rise against their rulers. His troops were given very little food—they were expected to live off the countryside once they had landed.

Meanwhile, the terrified local inhabitants had fled inland, leaving all their possessions behind them. Messengers had sped eastwards, and by 11 o'clock on Thursday morning a small defence force had gathered. Their total number was less than half that of the Frenchmen and there was no chance of any reinforcements for days, perhaps weeks.

Once they had landed, Tate and his troops advanced inland and placed guards on the main roads. The rest of his force was divided into smaller bands and ordered to find horses and carts to transport the guns and ammunition inland. Unfortunately for Tate, his half-starved convicts were more concerned with satisfying their appetites than finding transport, so they plundered every house within reach.

Now it happened that a smuggling boat had been wrecked off the coast a week earlier, and every cottager had salvaged a barrel of wine. The soldiers were delighted with the wine and food they found, and by the evening the effects of over-eating and heavy drinking had wiped out every trace of discipline. Tate was left with a rabble instead of an army. But, on Thursday afternoon, no one, not even General Tate himself, knew that.

By that time, the local people had been roused to fury by the tales of shooting and looting and had started to come back. The people of St David's stripped the lead off their cathedral roof and melted it down for bullets. Every countryman seized his scythe and marched towards the French. It wasn't only the men, either—Jemima Nicholls, a large woman who was a shoemaker from Fishguard, took a pitchfork and went hunting Frenchmen. Finding twelve of them in a field, she promptly arrested them and marched them to jail in Fishguard at the point of her pitchfork.

Hundreds of country people moved towards the invasion point, crowding the tops of the surrounding hills. From a distance the women in their Pembrokeshire costume of red cloaks and tall, black felt hats looked not unlike British Infantry soldiers who wore red coats and black felt hats.

Then someone had a brilliant idea, and, in a moment, 400 Welsh women were raiding every nearby house for pokers or staves. They marshalled themselves into ranks like soldiers, put their pokers on their shoulders like muskets and boldly marched over the brow of a hill and into full view of the French. Over the top of the hill they marched, rank behind rank. As the leaders dropped out of sight lower down the hill, they doubled smartly back behind the hill, where they couldn't be seen. Then they joined the end of the line of women to march over the top of the hill again.

To Tate and his officers, watching from a distance, it looked like

D

an unending line of British redcoats coming to the relief of Fishguard. To the grinning husbands and sons watching the puffing and panting that went on behind the hill it seemed impossible that such a mad scheme could work. Darkness fell on the lines of sweating women, and the men moved in to support their tottering wives. Had the trick worked?

At 9 o'clock that night, the French force surrendered. The bluff had worked. General Tate was no coward and he had a deep hatred of the British. But the indiscipline of his men, and the "thousands of troops" he thought he saw coming up as British reinforcements combined to compel his surrender. Britain had been saved from the ravages of Tate's horde of locusts by the courage and imagination of a bunch of countrywomen.

Assembly

Let us close our eyes and think. Let us think about facing up to danger. When the news of the French invasion came, the local people ran away. But then they stopped, thought about it, and returned. The odds were very much against them, but these ordinary people, armed with pitchforks against guns, marched towards the enemy forces and found, to their amazement, that they gave in.

They found that when they faced the danger it didn't look half as bad as when they ran away from it. Is this true of all unpleasant things? If we put off dealing with something unpleasant, does it get better or worse? Is it better to face up to unpleasant things, however much we dread them, or to run away from them?

Classwork

Tell us about: Have you ever been faced with a difficult situation which you have dreaded, and then found, when you came to it, that it wasn't half as bad as you thought?

Do you know of anyone who has refused to face up to a situation and so made it much worse for himself?

Discuss: a. "Procrastination is the thief of time."

b. You have just discovered that your best friend has been in the habit of stealing money from coats left in the cloakroom. What will you do?

Find out: Look at a map and find the places mentioned in the story. Trace Tate's route from France.

Group improvisation: The panic-stricken inhabitants of a small Pembrokeshire village are preparing to flee because they have heard the news of the looting and shooting by Tate's troops. Improvise the scene which leads up to their decision to turn round and face the threat.

Before you start, make sure you know who and what you are, your age, whether or not you have children, possessions, etc. Your reactions will depend on the character and background of the person you are "being".

Individual work: You are a boy or girl living near the Pembrokeshire coast at the time of Tate's invasion. Write a letter to your cousin in London describing your experiences.

15

Hans and the Company of the White Rose

By 1936, Hitler had complete control of Germany. All his opponents were murdered, and everyone who criticized him was beaten up and imprisoned. Children were brought up to believe that Hitler was almost a god, that everything he did was right, that his Nazis were the master race and must rule the world. They were told that the Jews were less than human, only good for slave labour.

The Jews were first humiliated, then hunted like animals, sent to concentration camps, or herded into slave labour camps and worked until they dropped. No one seemed to care, or, if they did, they were too frightened to do anything. Anyone who helped a Jew was also sent to a concentration camp.

One day in 1942, a German troop train, on its way to the Russian front, stopped for a few minutes outside a little station. Nearby, a group of slave women and girls were working on the embankment. The yellow Star of David sewn on their tattered clothes showed that they were Jews. They were haggard, grey, half-starved creatures, swinging heavy, steel picks almost too heavy for them to lift.

Nearest to the train was a young girl, pathetically thin with delicate hands and a beautiful, intelligent face. She paused for a moment to straighten her aching back, and noticed a soldier in the hated, grey, Nazi uniform climb out of one of the carriage windows. He came close to her. Fearfully she wondered what new humiliation she could expect. Then he took a tin out of his pocket, his emergency ration of chocolate, nuts and raisins which every soldier carried in case he was cut off from supplies. Hesitantly he held it out to her. With a flash of pride, the girl drew herself upright, took the tin, and threw it on the ground at his feet.

The soldier picked it up and smiled shyly. "I just wanted you to have something pleasant," he said. He looked round. Some white flowers were growing in the grass on the embankment—wild marguerites. He picked one and, with a little bow, placed it at her feet with the emergency ration.

The train started to move. The soldier ran after it and swung himself up. As he scrambled in through the window he looked back. The girl was standing where he had left her, staring after him. The wild marguerite was in her hair.

For one moment, before her inevitable death, that girl had been touched by someone who cared. Who was he—this German soldier who risked disgrace and imprisonment to bring a moment's pleasure to an unknown girl?

His name was Hans Scholl. He was twenty-four years old and a student of medicine at Munich University. Like everyone else, he had to do military service. In term time he studied to become a doctor, and during the holidays he was sent to fight at the front. It was on his journey to the Russian front that he gave the flower and emergency rations to the unknown girl. This was a simple action but, in the conditions that existed then, it was almost unbelievable that anyone could risk so much for so little.

Like most boys of his age Hans had joined the Hitler Youth Movement because he wanted more than anything else to work for the good of his country. Gradually, however, he began to see through the glamour of the Party, and by the time he reached his early twenties he had come to realize that Hitler and his Nazis were evil. He was not alone in feeling this. Many thousands of Germans would have agreed with him, but he was one of the few people in Germany at that time who felt he had to do something about it no matter what happened to him.

Hans Scholl started to write and distribute leaflets calling on the German people to resist the Nazis. He and his friends, calling themselves the "Company of the White Rose", worked in secret, turning out thousands and thousands of leaflets to distribute throughout the towns of southern Germany. They knew that sooner or later the Gestapo, the German secret police, would catch up with them, but they went on with their task as long as they could, printing leaflets and painting slogans like "Down with Hitler" and "Long Live Freedom" on the walls of Munich.

Hans could have escaped to Switzerland as the Gestapo came closer and closer to identifying him, but fleeing would have been a confession of guilt and the authorities would have arrested all his family and friends; so he stayed.

In 1943, together with his young sister, Sophie, and a friend, he was beheaded by the Nazis. Before he laid his head on the block he cried out, so loudly that it echoed round the prison, "Long live freedom." No one who heard that cry, whether they were warders or prisoners, ever forgot it.

Assembly

Let us close our eyes and think. Let us think about speaking out for what is right. Have we the courage to say and do what we know to be right even though the people round us do not agree? Are we brave enough to speak out as Hans did? *We* may have to face scorn and dislike. *He* had to face torture and death.

It is important to speak out for what is right and just in the little things of life as well as in the big things. Do we stay silent when something we know is wrong is being done?

Let us spend a moment in quiet thought about the German boy, his young sister and their friends who had the courage to stand up for what was right even though it cost them their lives.

Classwork

Tell us about: *a.* a time when you found it difficult to stand up and speak out.

b. a time when you, or someone you know, stayed silent "because it was easier".

Discuss: "Hitler was an extremist of the Right. Stalin was an extremist of the Left. Their methods were very similar and equally unpleasant for the people they ruled, but they *did* make their countries strong and powerful."

Is there any possibility that a similar kind of ruler could take over in this country?

Find out: *a.* What does "inflation" mean?

b. How did inflation in Germany help to bring Hitler into power?

Group improvisation: Divide into groups of about 10. Imagine this country is ruled by a "Hitler". Let's call him "Kilter". Most people believe that Kilter is a good ruler. They think his methods are justified because he has been able to feed the poor, to build good roads, and provide jobs for everyone.

Two of your group now believe that Kilter's methods are inhuman and disgusting. They have printed leaflets saying so which they have been distributing in a large area for some time.

The scene is set in a railway carriage. All the passengers believe passionately in Kilter, except for one, who is a resistance worker with a suitcase full of leaflets which he plans to hand over to his colleague at some time during the journey. Unfortunately, something happens which arouses the suspicion of one of the passengers. Take the scene from this point. (Don't forget to plan it well before you start. The scene should grow in tension from a fairly low-key start, in a series of "steps" till you reach the most exciting point just before the end.)

Individual work: *a.* A boy has been severely punished for something you know he did not do. No one knows you could clear him. To do so would mean getting yourself into trouble.

Write a description, in prose or free verse, of your feelings when you meet the boy.

       b. Prepare a leaflet of the kind printed by the resistance group to expose some of Kilter's more unpleasant policies. You may use drawings, cartoons and anything else you consider suitable to get your message over.

16

Atlantic Crossing

Teddie Brown was an engineer. Quiet and rather serious, he was not the sort of fellow who dreamed of being mobbed by schoolboys or pelted with flowers by thousands of people who had waited for hours to see him. Yet, at the age of thirty-five, to his great amazement, this actually happened to him.

During the First World War, Arthur Whitten Brown served as an observer in the Royal Flying Corps. Shot down in 1916 he was injured in the crash. Although he received excellent treatment in a prisoner-of-war camp, he was a cripple and in constant pain for the rest of his life.

After the war, the *Daily Mail* newspaper offered a prize of £10,000 to the first team to fly non-stop across the Atlantic, from Newfoundland to Ireland, a feat which required considerable skill and courage. To our eyes, aeroplanes of those days look as if they were held together by glue, bits of string and lots of luck. They were very slow, compared with modern planes, and could not fly very far before coming down for refuelling. The Vickers Aircraft Company was one of several to compete for the prize. They adapted a Vimy bomber, and had an excellent pilot called Jack Alcock. Teddie Brown became his navigator.

When they got to Newfoundland, Alcock and Brown found there were no airfields. Rocks had to be blasted and trees uprooted to make a take-off strip. Then gales kept them land-bound for weeks. At last, on 14 June, 1919, the twin-engined Vimy bomber, a frail biplane with an open cockpit, trundled drunkenly down the field and, at the last moment, dragged itself into the air. They were off!

All went well at first, but then things started to go wrong. They flew into a bank of fog which cut off all visibility. Then the radio generator failed, so they were cut off from the rest of the world. Two hours after take-off they were still climbing slowly through the thick cloud, when there was a terrifying banging from the starboard engine. A piece of exhaust pipe had come loose. Soon the heat from the exhaust fumes burnt it off and the engine pumped gas, heat and flames straight into their slipstream. The noise was deafening, but the engine still worked.

Two hours later they were still in thick fog. Then the battery which gave the power to heat their flying suits failed, and they began to feel the cold really badly. It was dark and they were still in the clouds, but they desperately needed a sight of the stars so that they could work out where they were. They climbed and climbed. Flames flickered from the broken exhaust, and were reflected back by the thick white mass all round them, as if they were travelling in a capsule of fire. At last, the stars appeared above, and Brown worked out that they were halfway across the Atlantic.

They flew steadily on until, just before dawn, they ran into a bank of cumulo-nimbus cloud, the kind even modern pilots avoid because they are full of electricity and dangerous air currents. At once the plane went crazy, bucking out of control and throwing itself about like a mad thing. Then the engine stalled. They went into a spin—down and down—lower and lower. When the altimeter, which told them how high they were flying, read less than one hundred feet, they fell out of the cloud into clear air. Brown glanced to the side and saw Atlantic rollers where the sky should be. Hastily Alcock righted the plane, and they skimmed over the waves until Brown looked at the compass and saw they were heading straight back for Newfoundland! Alcock roared with laughter and swung the plane back on course.

Slowly they regained height, but even at 6,000 feet they were still in cloud. Then they struck a bank of rain. As they climbed, the rain turned first to hailstones, which cut their skin, and then to snow. At 8,000 feet, the air intakes of the engines were blocked with snow. They had to do something about it quickly or they would drop from the sky. Alcock had his work cut out keeping the plane level, so Brown climbed out of the cockpit on to the wing. Battered and freezing in the icy wind he clung with one hand to a strut and leaned forward to scrape the ice and snow away with his clasp knife. Then he scrambled back into the cockpit and repeated the performance on the other side. Six times Teddie Brown, in agony from his crippled leg, climbed out on the wing, first on one side, then on the other, to clear the engines.

That wasn't the end of their difficulties, but at long last they sighted the Irish coast and headed for a pleasant-looking flat green field. Too late, they realized it was not a field but a bog. The plane touched down and promptly stood on its nose! Both men were thrown forward but were unhurt.

After sixteen hours in an open cockpit, they had crossed the Atlantic Ocean, which was, at that time, an incredible feat. When they landed in England they were given a hero's welcome. Men, women and children thronged to honour their courage and endurance—as we still do today.

Assembly

Let us close our eyes and think. Let us think about overcoming physical weakness. How easy it is to say, "I can't do that because I'm not strong enough," or, "Can I be excused P.E. because I don't feel well?" While it is only common sense to look after our health and follow doctor's orders, it's sometimes only too easy to make excuses for ourselves. We all do it— adults as well as young people.

Teddie Brown never allowed the pain in his crippled leg to stop him from doing what he felt was necessary. Are we always going to let our minor aches and pains stop us from doing what we know we ought to do?

Classwork

Tell us about: anyone you know who has a physical disability. How does he or she cope with it?

Discuss: It is said that the present generation lacks stamina. We fuss about our health and stay off work where there is no need to. Do you think there is any truth in this?

Find out: a. How many man hours are lost to industry in any one year as a result of colds and 'flu and absenteeism? (The public library should be able to help.)

b. Analyse the absences over one term of the members of your class.

Group improvisation: An experiment. Can you imagine what it is like when every movement you make shoots pain through your body? It is difficult unless you have actually had that experience. Find some sharp pebbles and put them in your shoes. (Don't cheat. The experiment will not work unless it really hurts.) Now try walking about the room. At first some people may laugh as they stagger about, but very soon they will find it is no joke. Carry on until you find the best way of coping with the pain. Don't wriggle the stones into a comfortable position in your shoe. Try to find the best way of walking so that you still feel the pain but it becomes bearable.

Sit down and analyse your experience. What effect did it have on your movement, on your temper and on your attitude towards other people?

Would your life be the same if movement was always so painful? Would you be the same person?

Divide into groups and discuss your experiences. Now think of anyone you know who has rheumatoid arthritis, which means that they are in considerable and constant pain. Prepare a short scene which shows how for such a person an ordinary task can become an ordeal, and how lack of understanding in other people can add to their difficulties.

Individual work: Prepare a three-minute talk to be given to the rest of the class on one of the following:

      a. the special Olympic Games held for handicapped people,

      b. the Thalidomide tragedy,

      c. rheumatoid arthritis—the causes, the research to find a cure and what we can do to help,

      d. spina bifida—the causes, the research to find a cure and what we can do to help.

17

Dick Whittington

One bitter winter day long ago in London, a group of boys ran down a narrow street leading to the river Thames. They were apprentices learning the trade of making fur caps, and part of their work was to clean and wash the skins used to make the caps. The only suitable place for doing this was on the bank of the river.

Leaving the shelter of the houses, the boys emerged on to the river bank and shivered as they met the full blast of the east wind. In the summer, scouring the skins wasn't such a bad job, but today, as the wind screamed up the Thames and froze the marrow in their bones, it required considerable fortitude to break the ice and plunge their arms again and again into the water below. Only the knowledge of the beating they'd get from their masters for work left undone drove them grimly on with their task.

People passed, heads down, bundled up in warm cloaks, hurrying to get home and out of the cold. No one glanced twice at the boys. They were an everyday sight, taken for granted by everyone who knew London in the fourteenth century.

A tall man, richly dressed in a fur-lined robe, came striding by. He hesitated when he noticed the boys kneeling by the river and asked, "Why are you scouring skins in weather like this?"

"'Cos we've got to!" one of the boys snapped, his chapped hands raw and bleeding. "You don't think we enjoy it do you?—sir!" he added hastily as he glanced up and took in the impressive appearance of the stranger.

The man sucked in his breath as he saw the state of the lad's hands. "Do you have to do this every day?" he asked the boys.

"Every day, summer and winter," they said. "It's worse when there's a high wind—you loose your footing see, and if you fall in—"

The man nodded grimly. There were far too many drownings on the river. "This is a disgraceful practice," he said. "I shall see that it is stopped. Good day to you." He swung round and strode away.

The boys looked at each other and shrugged. What could he, or anyone else, do to stop it? Disgraceful or not, it had been the practice to send apprentices to scour skins in the river every day for as long as anyone could remember. It would take more than one man's disapproval to stop it.

But the apprentices were wrong. When this particular man made up his mind that something was wrong, nothing in the whole city of London could stop him putting it right, for this was Richard Whittington.

Dick Whittington is a name that everyone knows. He was an ordinary man who so touched the hearts of the people he lived among that they loved to talk about him and tell their children stories about him. These stories were passed on from parents to children for 500 years, until today the true story of Dick Whittington is almost hidden under a fairy tale.

The true story is that he was the third son of Sir William Whittington of Pauntley in Gloucestershire, who followed the custom of the day by apprenticing his son to a respectable merchant who would teach him how to earn his living. In London, Dick served his seven-year-long apprenticeship with Sir Ivo Fitzwarren who was a mercer, or silk merchant. He became very good at his job and, in due course, set up in business on his own.

Over the years, Whittington became a very wealthy man. He was noted for his honesty, his integrity and his generosity. He was so respected by the townspeople that he became their Lord Mayor on four different occasions, something quite unheard of before or since! He seems to have been the sort of man who could never turn his back on anything that needed doing. He noticed that travellers coming into London through Cripplegate were thirsty from the dusty roads and had nowhere to get a drink. (Drinking water had to be bought in London in those days.) So he had a water tap installed where they could drink freely. The king borrowed vast sums of money from him to pay the soldiers in the English army. When the time came for the repayment of the debt Whittington realized that the king was in difficulties because of the great expenses of the French war. So he threw the bills on the fire and cancelled the debt.

Dick Whittington remembered the young apprentices on the river bank. When he became Lord Mayor, he passed a decree which prevented the fur cap makers from sending their apprentices to the river in either very cold or very stormy weather. And he made sure the decree was obeyed!

Whenever he saw a need, Dick Whittington did his best to fulfil it. He saw that St Bartholomew's Hospital was badly in need of repair, so he supplied the money to rebuild it. He provided almshouses for the poor and a college and library for scholars. Often his kindness to people was only discovered by accident. He preferred to keep his good deeds secret.

This was the real Dick Whittington. Parts of the pantomime story are certainly true. He really did marry Alice Fitzwarren, daughter of his old master, and lived happily with her. But, though it may be as a fairy tale hero we remember Dick Whittington now, the real reason that his name has come down to us over 500 years has nothing to do with fairy stories. The real reason is quite simple. He was loved by everyone who knew him because he was kind and generous and thoughtful—not bad reasons for being remembered.

Assembly

Let us close our eyes and think. Let us think about looking to see what is needed in the world around us. Dick Whittington did not wait until he had money and power before he helped people. He looked around, saw what was necessary and then did it.

How can we use our resources of energy, of strength, of youth and enthusiasm to help those in need? Let us spend a moment thinking of people who could do with a little help—help that perhaps we could give.

Classwork

Tell us about: a. people you know who could do with some help.

b. any time you (or someone you know) have spent time and trouble helping a person who was not a member of the family.

Discuss: Dick Whittington could *see* that the boys by the river needed help. How else can we find out about people in need?

Find out: what living conditions are like in Bangladesh.

Group work: Today there are so many people in need, it is not easy to decide whom to help. Divide into groups to discuss the following situation which is based on an actual case in the 1970s. Appoint a spokesman to report your views to the class.

Doctor X works for a charity organization with only a limited amount of money. He is sent to a semi-tropical island which has been devastated by a hurricane and a tidal wave. The survivors include 600,000 children. Of these, 30,000 need hospital treatment. (The only hospital has fifty beds but *no* nurses.) Almost all of the children suffer from worms and diarrhoea. There are few clean water supplies, and food is very scarce.

Doctor X has four other doctors and two health visitors to help him. He has only enough money to do *one* of the following:

a. Spend all the money on food and give a little to everyone until the money runs out.

b. Build a large hospital, find foreign nurses to run it and cure the worst cases (30,000 of them).

c. Ignore the worst cases and prevent the half-starving from becoming worse (360,000 of them).

d. Infected water and dirty conditions cause diarrhoea. A person with diarrhoea cannot absorb the food he eats. So the doctor can concentrate on improving water supplies, and go into the homes to train the mothers in good hygiene. (There are over a million people on the island and only seven in the medical team.)

What else could Doctor X do that would ease his task and cost little extra money?

Individual work: *a.* Write an essay discussing how you think charity money should be used: a little to every disaster area, or all to one; concentrating on the relief of suffering *now* or taking a long term view.

    b. Write a story about a boy or girl who is determined to find someone he or she can help. Think of some of the funny or embarrassing moments which might arise before he or she finds someone who appreciates his or her efforts.

18

Clara Barton and the Little Six

In the spring of 1884, the Ohio river rose till it burst its banks. People who lived along the banks of the Ohio and Mississippi rivers were used to floods, but this was worse than usual. In places the Ohio spread out till it was thirty miles wide. When the floods were at their height, a cyclone or wind-storm struck, and it swept along the entire length of the river leaving 400 miles of devastation in its wake. America woke up to the fact that thousands of people, the survivors, were left stranded and destitute. Everyone was shocked. Everyone wanted to help. But no one knew how to set about it.

Fortunately one person did know. Her name was Clara Barton. Two years earlier, she had founded the American Red Cross, which was dedicated to helping the victims of wars and disasters. She looked a fragile little lady in her long skirts and high button boots, but she had the mind of a field marshal! Intensely practical, her methods were simple: first get to the disaster area, then find out what was needed and supply what was necessary.

On the Ohio, people were homeless, cold and hungry. The government undertook to send food, so Miss Barton decided the Red Cross must supply coal and clothes to keep the people warm. Arriving in the area she found all roads had been washed away. So she hired a crew and a boat, loaded up with coal and boxes of clothes, and sallied out on to the swollen Ohio, weaving from bank to bank leaving supplies at each village.

Next, little Miss Barton loaded the boat with timber, hired carpenters and off they went again. They would stop for about three hours at each place on the bank where a farmhouse had been. There they would build a solid, one-roomed house stocked with furniture, bedding, clothes, food and farm tools ready for the next season, and they would leave a family warming themselves at their new fireside.

By this time, all America had heard of Miss Barton and her boat which flew the strange flag, a red cross on a white background, and many people had sent money to help the relief work. In the town of Waterford, a long way from the Ohio, there were six children (the youngest only seven years old and the eldest twelve) who wanted desperately to help the flood victims. They decided to put on a public concert. They organized it entirely themselves and made fifty-one dollars and twenty-five cents. They sent the money to the Red Cross and asked that it should be "put where it would do the most good."

In the midst of the incredibly complicated distribution of relief supplies and the administration of the tremendous amount of money now pouring in from all over the country (over 175,000 dollars), Miss Barton stopped, read the letter which was signed "The Little Six", and carefully put the fifty-one dollars and twenty-five cents on one side. That would not be put in the general fund, she decided. It was the result of a special effort and must be used for something special.

One day Miss Barton's boat stopped at a place beside the river bank where the wooden posts sticking up through the mud showed where a house had once stood. Higher up the bank was a barn which had not been swept away in the flood. Holding up her skirts, and with the mud oozing over the tops of her boots, Miss Barton scrambled up the bank towards it. There she found a woman and six children, the eldest a teenage boy and the youngest a two-year-old baby girl. The children were cleanly dressed in ragged clothes, and the barn floor was swept and tidy. Obviously this little family was determined not to squat down in despair even if they had lost their home and belongings.

The father of the family had died two years before. Mrs Plew and the children had kept their little smallholding going with a couple of horses, three cows, some pigs and some chickens, and had managed to make a decent living. Then, in the following spring, the Ohio had flooded, drowning the two horses and driving the family from their home. When the waters had subsided they had returned to their home but, in the wake of the floods, came swine fever and all but three of their pigs died. The next year, 1884, the floods came again, worse than ever. Mrs Plew packed all the furniture into the attic of their house and moved her family to the safety of the barn which was higher up the bank. They lived there for days, hoping that when the spring floods subsided they could move back. But before that could happen the fearful storm struck, whipping the waters to fury, overwhelming whole towns and flattening everything in its path. When the children looked out next morning there was nothing but grey water where their home had been.

Miss Barton was touched by the courage and determination of the

E

Plew family. Here, she felt, were six children whom the "Little Six" would be glad to help. So she handed over the hard-earned money sent by the unknown children of Waterford, and added enough to make it up to a hundred dollars. For the first time, Mrs Plew gave way to tears, but they were tears of gratitude and relief. She now knew that with the help of the Little Six her six children would have a warm home for the winter.

Before she left, Miss Barton asked what they would call their new house when it was built. Mrs Plew smiled. "We'll call it 'The Little Six'," she said, and probably the house called "The Little Six" which was built at Red Cross landing on the Ohio river is there to this day.

Assembly

Let us close our eyes and think. Let us think how every little helps. When we hear of disasters happening in distant places we find it difficult to realize quite what it means. "And anyway," we say, "what can I possibly do to help? Anything I could afford to send would be just a drop in the ocean. It wouldn't do any good. There's no point in bothering."

Even today, relief funds depend on ordinary people like us giving contributions. No one is going to have time to put our pennies on one side for a special purpose as Miss Barton did, but *all* the food and supplies are special to the people who receive them. Our pennies may buy milk for a sick baby or medicine to cure someone of cholera.

Let us pause for a moment and be thankful that our lives are free from the terrors of earthquake, tidal wave and hurricane, and think what it must mean for those who have to face these dangers.

Classwork

Tell us about: a. any work you know that the Red Cross does today, or any charity for which you have collected money, or relief work done by charities other than the Red Cross.

b. any experience you may have had of floods.

Discuss: Some people feel angry because all the money they give to charity does not reach the disaster victims. All charity organizations have expenses (rent, salaries, publicity, etc.). Would you like your money to go to an organization which was run by unpaid, idealistic volunteers, or one which was run by salaried, trained professionals?

Find out: about the T.V.A. (Tennessee Valley Authority). Look it up in the encyclopedia or in the books on America in the school library. Find out about this ambitious programme to prevent devastating floods in part of the United States of America. Will it prevent floods on the Ohio and Mississippi?

Group improvisation: Divide into "family" groups. The time is the present day and the place a village somewhere on the south-east coast of England.

It is the middle of a night of severe storm and the village is asleep. There is a strong onshore wind and an exceptionally high tide. The local constable is alerted by the coastguard, because the sea wall has been breached and the village is in danger of severe flooding. The villagers are roused and organize themselves into parties to repair the sea wall, make sandbags, get children to high ground, prepare emergency first-aid stations and sleeping quarters, evacuate farm animals, make hot soup and tea for the workers suffering from cold and exposure, etc. Plan your work exactly as if you were rescue services preparing for a real emergency.

Individual work: a. Write an account of how you would organize a fund-raising campaign for your favourite charity.

b. Recently, the Save the Children Fund received letters every day from an anonymous donor. Each letter contained a postal order for 15p or 20p, and a note saying, "please accept this donation". This went on for some time, until the total reached over £76. Make up a story telling who you think the donor was and how he or she came to send the money.

19

Twm and the Highwayman

Twm was a rogue, there was no doubt about that. He was a highwayman, a horse-thief and goodness knows what else besides, but you couldn't help liking him in spite of all that. He wasn't exactly Robin Hood, stealing from the rich to give to the poor, but his victims were always people who richly deserved all they got.

For instance, there was the crooked horse-dealer who offered a price far below market value for a very fine animal. Its owner, who looked a simple country lad, did not seem anxious to sell. He shook his head and sighed. "I'm afraid the horse *does* have a fault," he said in his broad country accent.

The dealer grinned for he knew he was getting a bargain. He pressed the money into the reluctant hand. "What fault?" he said laughing. "Show me."

"All right," said Twm and slowly climbed into the saddle. "The trouble with this horse," he said, "is that she disappears!" He dug in his spurs, and horse, man and money disappeared down the road leaving the horse-dealer in a cloud of dust.

You couldn't help laughing at Twm, but trust him with £200 in gold—surely only a fool would do that? Sir John Wynne was not a fool. He had befriended Twm and he needed to get £200 to London to pay for some land he had bought. To the astonishment of his friends, Sir John asked Twm to take the gold to London for him.

Travel in those days was very slow and very dangerous. There were so many highwaymen and footpads that anyone travelling with money to London would be lucky to get there alive. However, Twm accepted the task and set off, looking every inch the simple country lad on his scrawny pony. At first the journey was uneventful. No thief seeing the poor clothes and skinny pony gave Twm a second glance. Then, one night, he put up at a lonely inn just outside Marlborough. During the night, he overheard the hostess of the inn talking to Tom Dorbell, a notorious highwayman. It was obvious they suspected Twm of carrying gold. As the window in Twm's room was very small, he could not get out through it. He thought he would be seen if he tried to escape by another route, so he went back to sleep.

Next morning, Twm let the hostess see him thrust a hand into a tear in the pony's canvas-and-straw saddle and bring out some gold and silver which he used to pay her. Then he rode off as fast as he could towards a large pond which he had noticed the previous night. Behind him he heard hoofbeats and a rough voice shouted out, "Halt or I'll fire!" Twm quickly jumped off his pony and threw the saddle into the middle of the pond. With a howl of rage, Tom Dorbell leaped from his horse and waded hastily into the pond after it. Quick as a flash, Twm jumped on the highwayman's fine horse and galloped off, the gold safely in his pocket.

He sold the horse in Marlborough at a fine profit, bought a pistol and continued on his way on foot, thinking he would be less likely to be attacked that way. All went well until he reached Hounslow Heath, almost within sight of London. Not knowing that Hounslow Heath had a dreadful reputation for robbers, Twm allowed himself to relax. He was taken completely by surprise when a footpad stepped into his path, gun in hand. There was nothing he could do. He would be shot before he had time to pull out the pistol in his waistband. Quaking with fear, Twm handed over the gold. "D—D—Don't shoot," he stammered. "Not right, is it, that I should die for the old master's gold?"

"Turn out your pockets, Taffy!" the thief ordered.

"R—R—Right you are, sir—at once sir." Hastily Twm pulled out his travelling money and added it to the gold. "Is it bullets you got in that gun?" He eyed it nervously.

The thief grinned. "That's right, Taffy, you be a good boy and I won't put one in you!"

Twm wailed in terror. "Oh no sir, don't put one in me, sir. You take the old gold, *oh!* But the master will kill me when he knows I lost his money." Suddenly his eyes brightened. "Oh sir," he cried, "You got a kind face sir. Would you be so very obliging as to put a bullet in my coat? Make it look like there was a great fight see. If the master thinks I fought for his gold, he won't beat me so hard."

The footpad laughed. "All right," he agreed.

Quickly Twm put his coat over a bush and scuttled out of the way. "Put a bullet in it now, there's a lovely man," he begged.

Bang! went the gun. "Oh darro, there's a lovely noise!" Twm clapped his hands in glee. "Put a bullet in the other side now, isn't it?"

Bang! went the gun again. The footpad laughed to see the simple country lad dancing with excitement at each shot, and, entering into the spirit of the game, he peppered the coat with shot.

"Now one through my hat," begged Twm. "The old master will give me a present for fighting so hard."

"No, I can't do that," said the thief putting away his gun. "I haven't got any more bullets."

Twm smiled sweetly. "Haven't you?" he said, pulling out his pistol. "Well I have, so give me back the gold and my money. And while you're about it, you'd better turn out your pockets. You can pay me for the coat you've just ruined." He left the footpad a poorer but a wiser man, and Sir John Wynne's gold reached its destination safely.

In the year 1559, on 15 January, Queen Elizabeth the First granted Thomas Jones, otherwise known as Twm Shon Catti, a full pardon for all his misdeeds. He lived to a good old age, a highly respected man.

Assembly

Let us close our eyes and think. Let us think about giving people a second chance. Twm was a highwayman and a thief. Sir John Wynne gave him a chance to prove that he could be trusted, and his faith in Twm was justified. How many times do we give people a second chance? How many times do we say, "That man has been in prison, he'll always be a thief." How many times do we say, about someone who has been our friend, "He, or she, let me down once, I won't give him a chance to do it a second time."

If we do not give people a second chance, what treatment can we expect when our turn comes? Think about it; think about it now.

Classwork

Tell us about: a time when you felt someone had let you down. Did you feel so hurt that it was difficult to give them a second chance.

Discuss: The usual punishments in British law are fines or imprisonment. Think of more effective ways of fitting the punishment to the crime in the following cases:

     a. Soccer hooliganism
     b. Wanton destruction of public parks
     c. Dangerous driving.

Find out: what is meant by, "She was put on probation", and, "He was given a suspended sentence".

Group improvisation: A large house in Bronson Street has been bought by a charitable society to convert into a Halfway House, or hostel for men who have just come out of prison. It is for non-violent, first-offenders who find it difficult to get jobs and accommodation on leaving prison and have no relatives to go to. They need six months or so to become adjusted to looking after themselves.

The inhabitants of Bronson Street have called a public meeting to protest against "ex-convicts" coming into their neighbourhood. They are afraid of the possible danger to their children and property and are concerned at the possible effect on the value of their property.

Choose three people to represent the case for the charitable society and three to put the case against it. Appoint an independent chairman who will keep order and tell people when they can speak. The rest of the class are the inhabitants of Bronson Street who have come to listen, to make up their minds and, finally, to vote for or against the project.

Individual work: *a.* Why do you think there has been such an increase in crime in recent years? Describe the methods you think should be used to overcome the crime wave.

b. Write a story called "Second Chance".

20

The Railway of Death

Most boys' comics have stories about war, exciting stories full of fighting and heroism and good comradeship. They are great fun to read, but they have little to do with real life.

This is a true story about the Second World War.

In 1942, the Japanese generals in Tokyo decided they needed a railway across Burma to transport their troops. The railway had to be built straight through the jungle under the most terrible conditions. The men who built it were virtually slaves. They were local peasants or coolies and Allied prisoners-of-war. For every mile of track built, sixty-four prisoners-of-war and 240 coolies died. In other words, each sleeper laid represented a man's life.

The Japanese generals demanded a railway in a very short time. The Japanese guards knew their lives depended on getting results, so they drove their slaves until they dropped. This is the true picture of war—humanity thrown aside in an insane drive for victory.

Bill Duncan and Tom Simpson were prisoners-of-war who worked on the Railway of Death, as it was known. They were friends who had already been through a great deal together. They had survived torture in Singapore, then innumerable beatings and near starvation on the railway. Through it all they had kept their courage. Even at the worst times, Tom would manage to crack a joke and make Bill smile. Then they were sent deep into the jungle to a camp at Takanum where cholera had broken out.

Cholera is a dreadful disease which is serious even when the victims are cared for in good hospitals where everything is done to help the doctors. In the prisoner-of-war camps, the doctors were working in terrible conditions with little water and no sanitation, let alone any drugs or medicines. Despite their heroic work, thousands of men died. The bodies were piled on top of huge pyres of wood and bamboo and burnt. This was the only way to prevent the spread of the disease.

One day when Bill and Tom were working on the railway embankment Tom collapsed, and Bill realized that he had cholera. Like all the prisoners, both men looked like living skeletons.

Tom could only have weighed five stone, but Bill was smaller and must have weighed only four stone, less than a healthy eight-year-old child. Nevertheless, he managed to pick up his friend's body and staggered with it to the Cholera Compound and the doctor.

For the next few days Bill lived in fear. How could Tom survive when so many had died? When he went to see his friend, they told him Tom had been moved to the Death House where the dying were placed. In an agony of fear, Bill raced across, but there was no sign of Tom. He couldn't be dead already. Frantically Bill ran to the next hut which was used as a mortuary to prepare the dead for cremation. Tom was not there, but had already been taken to the funeral fires.

"*No!*" Bill glared wildly. "Tom is *not dead!*" He raced towards the fires.

Pathetic bundles lay on the ground—but not Tom.

A pile of bodies lay ready for cremation. Like a madman, Bill searched through them. Fearfully the prisoners nearby backed away from him. There was no sign of Tom.

Bill glared round desperately. An insane fury possessed him. "Tom is *not dead!*" he shouted. Suddenly Bill saw him—lying on top of a pile of bodies, high on a funeral pyre, the flames already reaching up and lapping round his arms and legs.

"*Tom!*" Bill sprang forward. Stumbling, slipping, he climbed the pyre, hardly noticing the searing heat. He reached upwards and managed to touch Tom's hand which was hanging limply down. With a desperate effort, he grasped and pulled. Tom's body slid towards him and fell to the ground, where it lay like a broken puppet, the eyes wide and staring.

With the strength of desperation, Bill picked Tom up and carried him straight to the doctor. "Do something for him, sir," he shouted. "He isn't dead!"

The doctor looked at the body and then at the wild-eyed man who carried it. Compassion filled his eyes. Bill was obviously on the point of complete breakdown, and it would be cruel to refuse his plea. The doctor took Tom's wrist and put his finger on the pulse. Bill stopped breathing—moments passed. Suddenly a strange look appeared on the doctor's face. "My God," he said, "this man is still alive!"

It was a long time before Tom was really out of danger, but at last Bill was told he could go and see him. Tom lay on a rough wooden bed. He was still horribly weak and pale, but a spark of humour lit his eyes when he saw Bill. He eyed him for a moment, then he grinned. "Left it a bit late, didn't you?" he murmured.

Bill and Tom survived the war and, after a long period in hospital, were sent home to England. The returning prisoners-of-war all thought they had left the horrors of Burma behind them, but they hadn't. Every year, more and more of them succumbed to the physical and mental effects of their imprisonment, and many died. Bill spent a great deal of time in hospital. Tom's mind misted over so that his memories became more real to him than the people around him—and then he, too, died.

Unlike comics, true stories of the war don't often have a real, lasting happy ending.

Assembly

Let us close our eyes and think. Let us think about war. What is it really like? Think of stories you have read in comics or adventure books about war. Think of films you have seen about heroic deeds done in battle.

Now think of pictures of war victims in newspapers and on television news programmes. Think of the faces of the refugees.

Which gives the true picture of war?

Classwork

Tell us about: *a.* anyone you know who was in Burma during the Second World War.

b. anyone among your family or friends who was killed or injured in a war.

Discuss: *a.* Why do wars start?

b. Who does the actual fighting?

c. How can we stop wars happening in the future?

Find out: Make a list of all the criticisms people make of other countries or races, e.g. "I can't stand the . . ." or "You can't trust . . .", etc.

Now make a list of any criticisms made of the British by people in or from other countries.

Group improvisation: Green country and Blue country have a long history of mutual hate and war. At the moment there is peace, but a group of hotheads in Blue country have called a public meeting where they will try to persuade their fellow countrymen to go to war against Green country.

Divide into two groups, one larger than the other. The small group will be the hotheads, who should plan together the best methods of winning over their fellow countrymen to a war policy.

The larger group can split up into pairs or small family units. They are the ordinary people of Blue country, and must decide exactly who and what they are (old or young; married or single; how they earn their living; how a war would affect them; etc.). Take time to think about it, then go ahead.

Finish by taking a vote by a show of hands. Vote, not as you yourself would, but as the person you are "being" would vote.

Individual work   a. Write an essay on the subject "Wars will never stop until we learn to trust one another".

b. Look at pictures of refugees then write a story beginning "I am a refugee. I am afraid. I don't know what to do . . ."

21

Help!

In 1970, Mr and Mrs John Simpson and their five children lived at 16 Violet Street, Norwich. On Wednesday, 27 May, Mr Simpson decided that next day he would take his three-year-old daughter, Lindy, to visit relations in Ely. His wife worked the night-shift in a local factory and spent most of the day sleeping, but Mr Simpson decided that the three eldest children, Tracey, who was seventeen, Dawn, who was fifteen, and fourteen-year-old Tony could quite well look after young Derek, who was four. He told Tony to stay in the house next day and keep an eye on his little brother.

On Thursday morning, Mr Simpson woke Dawn, telling her to hurry and get up to look after Derek, who was then still asleep. At a quarter past nine, Mr Simpson took Lindy and left home for Ely.

When he returned at a quarter to two, he found his home burnt out.

What happened at 16 Violet Street that day between 9 o'clock and 1 o'clock? Certain facts we know. At twelve o'clock all was quiet. Upstairs, in the middle bedroom, Mrs Simpson was sleeping after her night's work. In the front bedroom Dawn and Tracey were both still in bed and asleep, having decided to take a day off work because they didn't feel well. Tony had gone out to play with friends, and four-year-old Derek was downstairs in the front room.

The Simpsons were camping enthusiasts and, in the corner of the front room, by the window, was a propane gas cylinder which they used for cooking. Derek was an adventurous lad and, like most four-year-olds, he liked to experiment. He found some newspaper and matches. He also found he could turn on the gas cylinder. A fire started which the four-year-old could not control. Derek panicked and ran away to hide himself in a corner of the back kitchen.

The fire increased. The heat from the propane gas was intense. Soon the whole room was ablaze. The flames and smoke spread upwards towards the bedrooms.

In the middle bedroom upstairs, Mrs Simpson woke coughing.

Smoke filled the room. She ran to wake her daughters in the front
bedroom. Tracey sprang to the window, flung it up and leaned out
to shout for help. Escape down the stairs was impossible. Thick,
choking fumes filled the room and it was becoming unbearably hot.
The window was too high to jump out. Their screams echoed up
the street. A neighbour, Mr Robert Harvey, tried to get in to help
the women, but was beaten back by the intense heat. He ran to get a
ladder.

Inside the bedroom it was almost impossible to breathe. The
women sat astride the window-sill, leaning far out, gasping for air.

At 12.25 two plain-clothes policemen, Detective Sergeant
Walton and Detective Constable Moss, heard the screams and came
racing down Violet Street. They saw the women and realized the
situation was desperate. Constable Moss tried to get in at the front
door but found it locked. The Sergeant ran to a nearby garage, told
them to call the fire brigade, then returned with two workmen to
help. The workmen ran round to see if they could get in at the back
of the house while the police forced open the front door, but were
driven back by the intense heat and smoke. No one could get in
without breathing apparatus. The roar of the flames was increasing
every second. There was no time to get a ladder. The downstairs
room was an inferno fed by the propane gas.

Constable Moss, with complete disregard for his own safety,
climbed on to its window ledge. The Sergeant stood behind,
helping him to balance. They yelled to the panic-stricken women
to climb out. Tracey hastily scrambled over the window-sill,
lowering herself till she hung by her hands. Her feet just touched
the Constable's shoulders.

"Let go!" shouted Walton. "I'll catch you."

Sobbing with fear Tracey did so and fell backwards, to be caught
and lowered safely to the pavement. Mrs Simpson followed, then
Dawn. Flames gushed out from the downstairs window and drove
them back into the street.

"Is there anyone else in there?"

Coughing and choking Mrs Simpson gasped that Derek must be
somewhere inside. One glance at the flames and smoke belching
from the front sent the policemen racing to the back of the house
where the two workmen had placed a ladder against the lean-to
kitchen and had scrambled up over the roof to the back bedroom
window, only to be driven back by the heat and smoke.

"There's a child inside," the Sergeant called to the workmen.
"Have you seen any sign of him?"

"No." The workmen looked sick. "The smoke . . . you can't breathe..."

There was a momentary lull in the roar of the flames. A faint sound reached them and they strained to hear it. It was a child sobbing—*but where?* Sergeant Walton ran towards the back door. Taking a deep breath, he entered the kitchen. It was like pushing through a solid wall of grey cotton-wool, hot and suffocating. Stooping low to the floor where the air was a little clearer he groped his way forward. His eyes streamed, his chest battled painfully with the poisonous fumes. Suddenly his outstretched hand felt a wall on his right, then another on his left—it was the corner of the room. Groping downward he felt a soft bundle—it moved. Quickly he scooped the child up in his arms and, with one hand on the wall, groped his way towards the door. As he emerged, choking and gasping, he heard a shout, felt the child taken from him, then hands helping him away to cool fresh air.

The fire brigade arrived and dealt with the fire. Mrs Simpson, Dawn, Tracey and Derek were all taken to hospital suffering from the effects of smoke and shock. Tracey had cut her knee in the panic to get out and had to have it stitched, but after treatment they were all allowed to leave hospital. They were very lucky.

Assembly

Let us close our eyes and think. Let us think about who will come and help us if we get into danger. In the newspapers we sometimes see pictures of people jeering at policemen. On radio and television we sometimes hear people sneering at the police. Let us always remember, as we look at these people, that, if *they themselves* get into danger of any sort they will scream for help—from the police! Don't you think this is rather strange?

Let us think for a moment of what life would be like if there was no police force, no one to protect us from thieves and muderers, no one to go to for help. It would be like living in the Dark Ages, when rich men could hire armies and poor people could be killed or made into slaves. Let us spend a minute in quiet thought.

Just think what that sort of life would be like.

Classwork

Tell us about: *a.* any experience you have had with fire, e.g. a chip pan going on fire, etc. Why did it happen?

b. any time you have heard of when a policeman helped someone in distress.

Discuss: *a.* Who was to blame for the fire at 16 Violet Street?

b. At one time mothers used to frighten their children into silence by saying, "The 'bobby' will come and get you!" What long-term effect would this have on the children?

Find out: *a.* Make a list of all the jobs our police do (e.g. delivering babies when there is no doctor, etc.).

b. Find out as much as you can about the work and the methods used by police in other countries.

Group improvisation: The scene title is "Move On". Divide into groups of about 10. A group of teenage football fans are talking and larking about outside a fish-and-chip shop. Two young policemen on patrol are anxious to prevent trouble starting, so they tell the lads to move on. One of the group resents this. The others act exactly as you think they would. Finish the scene as you think best.

Individual work: *a.* Make a collection of press cuttings showing the work the police do.

b. Imagine you are a young policeman (or the policeman's wife) who has had no weekends off for six weeks because there have been so many marches and demonstrations. One of the most important jobs of the police is to secure freedom of speech for *everyone* in Britain. You are one of a small force which has to secure freedom of speech at a rally held by people whose ideas you dislike. You know that a rival group plan to stop the rally, and you know you will be attacked with fists, feet and stones when you try to protect the people in the rally. Describe your feelings as you line up, arms linked with your mates, to try to stop the thousands of angry people getting through. You can use prose, verse or any form of "free writing" you like.

22

John Brown

John Brown lived in America over a hundred years ago. To understand his story, one needs to know a little about the way in which the country we call the United States of America grew up. To begin with it wasn't *one* country. It was a lot of little countries, or states, each ruled by a separate government, each with its different set of laws and each very proud of its independence.

Gradually these separate states began to realize that, though they would not dream of giving up their independence, there were times when it was a good idea to join together and act as one country. So they formed a federation, or union, with a federal government formed of representatives from each of the states. This Federal Government of these "*United* States" was responsible for things like trade with other countries, and for the army which protected them all from possible foreign invasion, but each separate State looked after its own people and had its own laws. So it happened that some States had a law which said that people could own slaves, and other States had a law which said that people could *not* own slaves.

There were slave States in the southern part of North America where the climate was hot, and negro slaves were needed to work on the cotton plantations, for example, in Florida, Georgia, Alabama and Mississippi. The Northern States of America, on the other hand, were free States.

Most slave owners were kind and considerate to their slaves, but some were not. Sometimes slaves would run away from their masters and try to cross into one of the free States or into Canada where they would be safe and free.

One man who was violently opposed to slavery was John Brown. In his youth he had helped runaway slaves to escape into Canada. Later he organized a league among negroes to help them protect themselves against the slave catchers who often pursued runaway slaves and tried to take them back by force.

He was an odd mixture, John Brown. To look at he was very like the photographs your grandmother may have of her father and grandfather—stern-faced men with bushy beards and high, white, stiff collars, the sort of men you'd never dare to contradict. John Brown must have been a bit like that. He was married twice and had twenty children!

He never made a success of business, though he tried in several different places. He finally settled in the State of Kansas at a place called Osawatomie.

Kansas at the time was a State where some people were for slavery (pro-slavers) and some were against it (anti-slavers). Brown, of course, worked to keep Kansas a free State. Unfortunately, he was so sure that his aim (to get rid of slavery) was a good, just aim, that he didn't think it mattered what he did to bring it about. He thought the end justified the means and, in some ways, he was no better than the pro-slavers. For instance, he was quite ready to kill if he thought it was necessary.

In Kansas, in 1856, tempers ran high and violence often broke out. In May, 1856, pro-slavery men attacked and burned the town of Lawrence. Two days later, Brown led a revenge raid on a pro-slavery settlement in Poltawatomie Creek and brutally killed five settlers there.

During the next year, Brown successfully defended the town of Osawatomie against raiders, and was nicknamed "Old Osawatomie Brown". There were a number of other small but bloody battles until, by 1857, Brown had come to the conclusion that the only way to stop slavery was to get an army and invade the Southern States.

Lots of people were against slavery and they helped John Brown, but not all of them realized what his plans were. They certainly did not think they involved rebellion and full-scale war!

Brown's plan was to get lots of guns and ammunition and arm the negro slaves, who would then rebel and fight for their freedom. He started collecting guns and ammunition, but it was a slow task. So he decided to get all he wanted in one big haul, and he conceived the daring plan of raiding the arsenal of the United States army, which was in Harper's Ferry in West Virginia. If he succeeded, they would have all the rifles and ammunition they needed and the army would have lost a good part of its reserves.

On the night of 16 October, 1859, Brown took a small party of only eighteen men (five of them were negroes), surprised the garrison and took over the arsenal. Their daring plan actually succeeded, but then things began to go wrong for them.

Brown expected the slaves to revolt and flock to join him, but they didn't. Instead the people of Harper's Ferry organized their militia and managed to trap Brown and his small force, together with some prisoners they had taken, in the fort there. Then, on 18 October, a force of United States Marines arrived under the command of Colonel Robert E. Lee.

Lee was an outstanding man. He was a Southerner who had actually freed all his own slaves. He was also a very good soldier and it didn't take him long to recapture the fort. Fifteen of Brown's men were killed. The rest were taken prisoner, including Brown himself, and handed over to the State for trial on charges of treason and murder.

Brown was convicted of treason and hanged on 2 December, 1859.

Two years later, the Civil War broke out between North and South. The ordinary soldiers didn't know all the reasons for that war, but the Northern soldiers did know that they were against slavery. So they fought and marched into the South and, to keep themselves in time as they marched, they sang—

"John Brown's body lies a-mouldering in his grave
But his soul goes marching on."

Assembly

Let us close our eyes and think. Let us ask ourselves if the end ever justifies the means. John Brown wanted all human beings to be set free from slavery. To achieve this he was prepared to kill other human beings. Was this right?

When we are trying to bring about something good, does it matter what means we use to get it?

When we are fighting passionately for a good cause is it easy to let enthusiasm run away with us and distort our sense of right and wrong? Let us think about John Brown quietly for a moment. Was he right?

Classwork

Tell us about: anyone you know, or have heard of, who does not care what he or she does in order to get what he or she wants.

Discuss: Is it often the *lazy* people who say, "Ah well, the end justifies the means"?

Find out: Look up John Brown and Robert E. Lee in the encyclopedia in the school library. Which of the two men would you have preferred to have as a friend? Why?

Group improvisation: The heavy flow of traffic on a main road cuts a village in two. The inhabitants have been told that there is not enough money available to build a bypass. They determine to stop all traffic in order to draw attention to their need. Divide into two groups. Group A is formed of villagers. Group B consists of motorists, etc., who all feel that they have an urgent need to continue their journey. Both groups passionately believe that they are right. Work out the situation.

Individual work: a. Prepare a talk on the life of a slave on a cotton plantation during the early nineteenth century.

b. Write a description of the feelings of a slave as he wakes up in the morning. Use verse, "free writing" or prose.

23

Spooks and "the Pimple"

In 1917, Lieutenant E. H. Jones, or Bones as he was usually called, was a prisoner of war at Yozgad, which was the Turkish punishment camp in the First World War. There were no escapes from Yozgad, for everyone knew that even an attempted escape would result in the whole camp being punished in such a way as to cause many deaths among the prisoners.

To relieve the monotony and take their minds off their hunger and cold, the prisoners invented many different games and were not above playing practical jokes on each other. Bones had a considerable reputation as a joker, but he excelled himself when he convinced his companions that he was a medium who could contact the Spirits of the Dead. Knowing Bones' reputation, his fellow officers set him elaborate tests to try and catch him out, but Bones was blessed with considerable intelligence and an incredible memory. What had started as a joke became, for him, a battle of wits which he took secret pride in winning.

Bones' spooks created a great deal of amusement and excitement for the prisoners, but all the time he was trying to work out some way to escape from Yozgad and prevent the Turkish Commandant from punishing the camp afterwards. He decided that the only safe way was somehow to get proof that the Commandant had actually helped him to escape. That proof could be left behind and used as blackmail. The Commandant would not dare punish the remaining prisoners if he knew they could expose him to his superiors. Unfortunately, though the Commandant was guilty of many crimes, helping prisoners to escape was not one of them.

None of the prisoners ever even *saw* the Commandant. The only contact they had with him was through the camp interpreter, a bouncy little man full of his own importance, who was known to live well on the contents of the parcels sent to the prisoners by their families. They called him "the Pimple". The Pimple was a cunning rogue, but Bones managed to lure him to a mock séance where, with the help of some friends, he convinced him the spooks were genuine and that he really could talk with the dead.

From the Pimple, Bones learned that the Commandant had been

hunting for £17,000 in gold which he knew had been hidden somewhere in the village of Yozgad at the beginning of the war. Bones decided he must convince the Turks that his spooks could find the gold. He remembered that one of the prisoners had discovered a rusty revolver half-buried in the ground. The gun was useless, but it could be used to bait a trap. Carefully they reburied the revolver, taking pains to see that the ground above showed no signs of disturbance.

A special séance was held. Bones went off into his pretended trance, and the "spook" spoke in a strange voice through his mouth, giving detailed instructions to the Pimple. "*Beware*," it warned. "The treasure is by arms guarded. *Take a companion*. First, find the arms—you will then be led to the treasure. Follow my instructions *exactly.*"

Next morning the excited Pimple met Bones. But, to the prisoners' disappointment, the companion the Pimple brought with him was not the Commandant but only the Commandant's orderly.

Jones pretended to go into a trance, then spoke in a deep, slow voice, "What—did—you—say?" He stared at the space behind the interpreter.

The Pimple spun round. "B—B—But there is no one there!" he gasped.

His eyes vacant and staring, Bones raised his arm and pointed. "*South!*" he shouted, and headed straight for the barricade.

"Let him through!" screeched the Pimple. The astonished sentry obeyed and the odd procession marched out. Bones led the plump Pimple and his perspiring friend up hill and down dale before returning to the prison compound, where they collected a crowd of grinning spectators.

Bones halted, then spun round on the exhausted Pimple. "Quick, light a fire," he ordered.

The Turks scurried round piling up kindling on the exact spot where the old gun lay buried. The flames sprang up. With eyes flashing and arms flung high, Bones stood over the blaze and, in a loud, unearthly cry, uttered a magic incantation.

Actually, it was a Welsh nursery rhyme. But, since the Turks didn't understand Welsh, it made a considerable impression.

"It is here—I feel it—there!" With a grand theatrical gesture, Bones pointed to the ground. "Get me a pick—*at once!*"

Like a flash, the orderly streaked away, found a pick and returned panting. Bones took it and plunged it into the centre of the fire. Sparks flew, then clods of earth, and then the butt of the revolver appeared. With a wild yell, Bones pointed at it, staggered, and fell in a dead faint.

It was a very good faint—so good that one of the spectators thought it was genuine and dowsed him with a bucket of cold water!

The Pimple and the orderly ignored everything except the hole. Triumphantly they pulled out the revolver, grabbed the picks and dug and dug and dug until they almost disappeared from sight. At that point, Bones decided to come back to life. "Oooh!" he groaned. "What happened?"

The Pimple scrambled out of the hole. "You have been in a trance," he beamed. "You found the arms which guard the treasure and we are digging—"

"*You* are digging?—oh no!" cried Bones. "You have ruined everything. The spook told you to follow instructions *exactly*. He did not tell *you* to dig. Now you have angered the spirits. Have you found the treasure?"

Dolefully the Pimple shook his head. "No, you are right. We must have angered the spook, for look, the hole is empty. We will do anything you say. We will not disobey again."

From then on, they followed the spook's instructions very carefully! Bones' plan worked. The Commandant was lured out into the open by the promise of gold. He was completely taken in by Bones and his partner Lieutenant Hill, who actually managed to take a photograph of the Commandant helping Bones. When they escaped from Yozgad, they left this photograph with the other prisoners to prove that the Commandant was involved, and so prevent him from punishing anyone. If you want to know exactly what happened, you must read *The Road to En Dor* by E. H. Jones.

Assembly

Let us close our eyes and think. Let us think about greed. The Camp Commandant was an intelligent, well-educated man, and so was the Interpreter. But they were also greedy. They allowed their greed for money to blind them to every other consideration. Jones and Hill played on this greed and led them by their noses so that they made complete fools of themselves.

There are times when we all dream of finding treasure, not buried in the ground but in the football pools, the bingo halls or the betting shops. It sometimes happens that people become blinded by the thought of the treasure they could win and start paying too highly for it—in *time* as well as in money.

There are times when each of us is greedy, when we want more than we have earned. It is good to be able to recognize this greed when we feel it. Then we can laugh at ourselves when we are tempted to spend too much time or money in bingo halls, or betting shops or in any other way of treasure hunting.

Classwork

Tell us about: a. any ways of "treasure hunting" you enjoy such as games of chance, competitions like "spot the ball", etc.

b. anyone you know who spends more time and/or money than he or she can afford in betting shops or bingo halls.

Discuss: You have won enough money to keep you in comfort all your life. You do not have to work. How long would you be satisfied with doing nothing?

Find out: Find Yozgad on a map of Turkey. Where were the Allies fighting the Turks during the First World War?

Group improvisation: Divide into groups of about 6. Choose one of the following scenes to work on:

a. Mary has just spent most of the week's housekeeping money on bingo. Improvise the scene where the family, fed up with a monotonous diet, realize what has happened.

b. Joe has lost a great deal of money by backing (heavily) the wrong dog. His children need warm coats for school and his wife explains that, because of rising prices, she needs more housekeeping money. Improvise the scene that leads to Joe having to admit what has happened. End the scene as you think best.

Individual work: a. Write an essay on the subject "Greed", pointing out how many different forms greed can take.

b. Write a play based on one of the improvisation scenes.

24

Danger!—Tide Race

If you hold a spoon under a running tap, the water will swirl round the bowl of the spoon and splash up into the air. Swansea Bay is spoon shaped; the outgoing tide runs round the coast from east to west, swirls round the bend and swishes off the end of the spoon at Mumbles Head only to collide headlong with the main body of water coming down the middle of the Bristol Channel. The result is called a "tide race", which is an area of very rough water indeed, with waves, often over ten feet high, going in every direction at once. When the wind blows from the east, it sets up a heavy ground swell which makes conditions at Mumbles Head even more dangerous.

At 8 o'clock on the morning of 12 April, 1972, Alun Bessette, wearing a wet-suit and a life jacket, stepped into his fifteen-foot-long canoe at Sketty, which is just outside Swansea, and pushed off from the shore. He paddled out into the bay but it was not long before he realized that conditions were not as good as he had thought. The weather was obviously deteriorating, so he turned for the shore. The east wind was setting up a heavy swell and whipping the tops off the waves. At 8.30, the canoe capsized throwing the boy into the water. Alun clung to the side and tried to right his boat, but found that conditions made it impossible. So he decided to swim for it and tow the canoe to shore.

A life jacket holds you up in the water making you bob about like a cork on the surface. It saves your life but makes it difficult to swim. Alun made little headway, and the wind and tide carried him westwards across the bay. In the distance, he could see Mumbles Head where he knew the tide race foamed and roared. Once in that, he wouldn't stand much chance of coming out alive.

The tide swept him past the village of Mumbles. Just ahead was the pier jutting out 300 yards into the bay, with the lifeboat station tucked in beside it. He was too far out to be heard from the shore, but there might be someone on the pier. Alun strained his eyes. Yes, there were fishermen. He shouted and waved, but the wind blew his voice away. He tried again and again. Suddenly one of the figures jerked to attention and pointed. There was a flurry of movement. One figure broke from the group and ran. The others crowded round the rail and shouted encouragement. There was no way they could get down to help him.

Derek Scott, the coxwain of the lifeboat, knew the coast like the back of his hand. He had already been awarded both the bronze and silver medals for courageous rescues of seamen in danger. He was at home when he heard there was a boy clinging to an upturned boat off Mumbles pier. Realizing there was very little time, he shouted to his wife to telephone the crew of the Inshore Rescue Boat and raced across the road to the beach. A dinghy lay with its outboard motor turned up over the stern. Praying it had enough fuel, Scott pushed it down the shingle to the water and jumped in. He swung the motor into position, started up, and headed for the pier.

"That way!" the fishermen shouted, pointing towards Mumbles Head. With a sinking heart, the coxswain realized the boy had already been swept on out of sight. By keeping close to the shore, just clear of the rocks, Mr Scott managed to avoid the worst of the broken water and made his way towards the Head, hoping to overtake the boy before he was drawn into the tide race.

The wind was blowing strongly from the east. Beyond the shelter of the headland he could see the confusion of waters. There were waves as much as ten feet high with the wind blowing off the foaming crests. The wind, the swell and the headlong collision of two strong currents caused a terrifying turbulence—and there, in the middle of it, was the boy.

It was obvious that Alun was exhausted. He couldn't last much longer. Even if his lungs kept free of water he could not survive the battering he was taking.

Derek Scott turned his little dinghy into the tide race. The waves caught it and tossed it high. Then the bows slid into a trough, deeper and deeper. Suddenly an oncoming wave ran under the bow and lifted it so high, so steeply, that the little boat seemed to stand up on its hind legs. Scott flung himself into the bows and pressed down with all his strength, just in time to stop the dinghy somersaulting bow over stern. With no time to think, he reacted instinctively as time and again the boat was about to capsize. The sea behaved as if a dozen giant hands were whipping it into a fury. It was impossible to tell from which side the avalanche of water would crash down on him next.

At last, the dinghy reached the boy. Desperately balancing the boat, Scott yelled to him to haul himself aboard. Alun was exhausted, quite incapable of such an effort. His life jacket had come loose and was not giving him the support he needed. Scott took a line and tied the boy to the dinghy. Then he unshipped the outboard motor and laid it in the centre of the boat. That left enough room to haul the boy aboard over the stern, always providing the boat stayed afloat. It was shipping water badly.

Derek Scott knelt in the stern, put his arms round the boy and tried to haul him aboard. The dead weight was too much for him. The dinghy was still being battered and tossed in every direction. Setting his teeth, the coxswain took a fresh hold. He held on tightly as they were tossed into the air, then, as the stern sank, he bent far out grasping as much of Alun's body as he could and dragging it towards him. As the next wave ran under the stern, Alun was lifted and tossed forward into the boat on top of the coxswain who crashed backwards onto the floorboards.

As soon as Scott had recovered, he pulled himself out from under Alun's body and staggered to the stern to fix on the motor—not an easy task. Grimly Scott struggled, succeeded, started up the motor, then headed out of the tide race.

As the battered dinghy emerged into calmer water it was met by the Inshore Rescue Boat. Alun was transferred to the larger boat. They recovered his canoe and set off for home. At five past ten, Alun was safely on shore after the most terrifying experience of his life.

Assembly

Let us close our eyes and think. Let us think about the courage we take for granted in our Lifeboat Service. Since the Lifeboat Service started, 95,000 men, women and children have been saved from drowning. Many lifeboatmen have given their lives in the attempt to save others.

We may live inland, we may never set foot on board a ship, but most of us visit the seaside and may, one day, have reason to thank the lifeboatmen. They have rescued children who drift out to sea in rubber dinghies, teenagers who have been cut off by the tide when exploring caves or rock climbing, pilots who crash in the sea, weekend fishermen whose outboard motors break down, and visitors who get washed off the rocks when the sea is high. Next time it may be one of us.

Let us spend a moment in silent thanks for those men who are prepared to risk their lives for us, just as Derek Scott did for Alun Bessette.

Classwork

Tell us about: a time when you have felt the power of the sea, either on your own body or by watching its effect on somebody or something else.

Discuss: What makes a lifeboatman? All are volunteers. Each boat has only one full-time crew member (the mechanic). The others may be fishermen, clerks, builders, printers, hotel workers, etc. Why do they do it? Would you do it?

Find out: a. what you should do if you saw someone in difficulties in the sea.

b. how to do mouth-to-mouth resuscitation. Everyone should know this, *but* learn from a proper instructor and *no one else* (the Red Cross and similar organizations can send demonstrator teachers).

Group improvisation: Divide into groups of 6–8. Think of different ways in which people can get into trouble at the seaside. Each group take *one* of these and work out a situation which would result in the Lifeboat Service being called out. (WARNING: Do *not* try mouth-to-mouth resuscitation on each other. It is dangerous.)

Individual work: a. On 23 December, 1970, a fifteen-year-old youth ran up to a group of fishermen and told them that his brother had been washed off the rocks at the harbour entrance. Write a story showing how this situation came about and how it ended. (Afterwards you may like to find out what really happened by reading the true account in *The Story of the Lifeboat*, published by the Royal National Life-boat Institution, West Quay Road, Poole, Dorset BH15 1HZ.)

b. Think of the immense power of the sea. Write a description which makes the reader feel this power. You might like to use a form of "free writing" or verse to get over the mood more vividly.

25

When It's Brave to Be Chicken

This story is based on a true case, though some details have been added.

It was the last day of the school holidays. Brian peered out at the moist, misty morning. "Tomorrow it's sure to be fine and sunny," he thought. "It always is the first day back at school." He crossed to the foot of the stairs. "Mum, I'm going to call for Gary," he shouted. "Bye!" The door slammed after him.

Upstairs a window was flung up and his mother leaned out. "Don't be late for your dinner," she warned. He dodged the shower of dust shaken from her mop and strolled down the street. At the corner he met his friend.

"This is Stuart," said Gary, jerking his chin towards a boy who was with him. "He's my cousin. He's staying with us."

Together the boys made their way to the common. For a while they amused themselves balancing on the top of an old stone wall, trying to push each other off. When they tired of that, they sat on the wall, feeling gloomy. There was nothing to do, and the thought of school the next day didn't help.

Brian stared across the countryside. On the one side were pasture and ploughed fields bordered by neat hedges; on the other, rolling heath with rough grass, bracken, clumps of brambles and a line of electricity pylons stretching from skyline to skyline. He knew every inch of it. There was nothing left to explore. "This place is a dump," he muttered. "There's never anything to do."

"It's better where I come from—" Stuart started.

"Oh, yes, you've got everything at your place, haven't you?" Gary was fed up with his cousin.

"Not everything," Stuart protested. "But when there's nothing else to do you can always go climbing. There's one place where they do rock climbing, you know, like you see on telly. I went climbing once—"

"Bet I could climb higher than you," muttered Brian.

"It's not as easy as you think," Stuart said quickly.

"Garn!" Brian laughed scornfully. The next moment the boys were arguing hotly, each sure that *he* was the best climber.

"Prove it!" Brian yelled at Stuart. "Go on, if you're so good, you show us!"

"How can I?" Stuart was surly. "You haven't got any rocks or decent trees or anything to climb."

"We've got that!" Brian pointed to the nearest of the long line of steel pylons which marched like ungainly giants, elbows stiffly out, white insulators hanging where hands should be.

Gary stared. "The electricity pylons! You're nuts! Those wires are dangerous."

"You don't have to touch the wires. Go on. You're so clever Stuart. You climb up that pylon, over the top and down the other side. I dare you!"

"I wouldn't be so daft!" Stuart stared at the pylon. "It's got a 'Danger' notice on it."

"You're chicken!" Brian sneered.

Gary flared up in defence of his cousin. "I bet *you* wouldn't do it anyway!"

"Yes I would!" Brian snapped.

"Go on then. I dare you!"

Brian's eyes glittered. "I'll do it if you will. I dare you to follow me."

"No!" Stuart protested. "Don't be daft, Gary".

"Chicken! Chicken!" taunted Brian. He turned, ran to the nearest pylon and started to climb. A few feet up from the ground he turned round, grinning, sure the others would be walking away. But he found Gary right behind him and Stuart was behind Gary. He turned back and pulled himself up to the barbed wire which was stretched across to prevent people climbing any higher. It wasn't easy to get past the wire but he managed it—and still Gary was behind him.

Brian set his teeth and climbed upwards, past the red "Danger" notice. Surely Gary wouldn't really follow, not all the way? The moment Gary and Stuart stopped, he could stop too. But he couldn't be the first to give up. His pride wouldn't let him.

Below him, Gary looked upwards. He knew they were being stupid. If only Brian would stop.

But Brian didn't stop. He went on towards the first of the cross-bars. There were three of them, six feet apart, holding white insulators from which the heavy wires drooped, before rising, in a slow curve, to the next pylon. The boys knew it was death to touch those wires, but they trusted in their ability to climb over without touching them. What they did *not* know was that there were 33,000 volts of electricity passing through those wires and, when the voltage is as high as that, you don't have to touch the wire—the electricity comes to you. In fact, it can jump quite a large gap.

That is what happend to Brian. One moment he was climbing, the next moment there was a sheet of flame as the electricity passed through his body and down to the ground. Brian was killed instantly. Gary was so badly shocked and burnt that he fell to the ground and was killed. Stuart was burned too and fell, but he did not have so far to fall and he survived.

When he was interviewed in hospital, Stuart was asked why he had been so stupid as to climb the pylon. He said: "I didn't want them to think I was chicken."

Assembly

Let us close our eyes and think. Let us think about foolish dares. Have we the sense to realize that it is sometimes brave to be "Chicken", that it sometimes needs more cold courage to face the sneers of our friends than to dash out and do the silly thing we have been dared to do?

When we risk our own lives, we also risk years and years of pain and sorrow for the people who love us. The parents of Brian and Gary still mourn their sons and will miss them every day of their lives. Have we the right to let our stupid pride condemn the people who love us to that kind of fate?

Classwork

Tell us about: a. a time when you were dared to do something silly,

b. about anyone you have heard of, or read about, who has made foolish dares.

Discuss: a. "It's always boys who make stupid dares—girls have got too much sense!"

b. "My life is my own, I can do what I like with it."

Find out: What is the voltage of the electricity supply in your house? Would it harm you if you touched a bare wire?

Group improvisation: Divide into groups of about 6. This is not going to be a planned play. It is an exploration. No one knows how or where it will end, except that one, or more, of the group will be challenged to do some kind of foolish dare. He or she must then choose whether or not to accept it.

Do not discuss anything. Sit down for a moment by yourself and think. Decide for yourself what sort of person is likely to become involved with foolish dares. Make up your mind to try and think, feel and behave like that person.

Now get up and start talking, listen to each other and reply *in character*.

Set yourselves a time limit, about three to five minutes is usually enough to start with. Then stop and discuss how and why things developed as they did. You may want to start again and repeat the experiment two or three times once you have developed confidence.

Individual work: The Electricity Board has commissioned you to educate the public in the dangers of high voltage cables and installations. (The Board will supply you with information if you ask for it.)

      a. Design a poster for mass distribution in schools.

      b. Write the script for a five-minute radio programme.

Page